CW00919116

BUDDHA STANDARD TIME

BUDDHA STANDARD TIME

Awakening to the Infinite Possibilities of Now

Lama Surya Das

HAY HOUSE

Australia • Canada • Hong Kong • India
South Africa • United Kingdom • United States

First published and distributed in the United States of America by:
HarperCollins Publishers, 10 East 53rd Street, New York, NY 10022.

First published and distributed in the United Kingdom by:
Hay House UK Ltd, 292B Kensal Rd, London W10 5BE. Tel.: (44) 20 8962 1230;
Fax: (44) 20 8962 1239. www.hayhouse.co.uk

Published and distributed in Australia by:
Hay House Australia Ltd, 18/36 Ralph St, Alexandria NSW 2015. Tel.: (61) 2 9669 4299;
Fax: (61) 2 9669 4144. www.hayhouse.com.au

Published and distributed in the Republic of South Africa by:
Hay House SA (Pty), Ltd, PO Box 990, Witkoppen 2068. Tel./Fax: (27) 11 467 8904.
www.hayhouse.co.za

Published and distributed in India by:
Hay House Publishers India, Muskaan Complex, Plot No.3, B-2, Vasant Kunj, New Delhi –
110 070. Tel.: (91) 11 4176 1620; Fax: (91) 11 4176 1630. www.hayhouse.co.in

Copyright © 2011 by Lama Surya Das

The moral rights of the author have been asserted.

All rights reserved. No part of this book may be reproduced by any mechanical, photo-
graphic or electronic process, or in the form of a phonographic recording; nor may it be
stored in a retrieval system, transmitted or otherwise be copied for public or private use,
other than for 'fair use' as brief quotations embodied in articles and reviews, without prior
written permission of the publisher.

The image on p. 202 is based on an original diagram that appeared in *One Peaceful World*
by Mishio Kushi and Alex Jack, St. Martin's Press, 1987.
Copyright © 1987 Michio Kushi and Alex Jack.

Interior design by Laura Lind Design

The author of this book does not dispense medical advice or prescribe the use of any
technique as a form of treatment for physical or medical problems without the advice of
a physician, either directly or indirectly. The intent of the author is only to offer information of a general nature to help you in your quest for emotional and spiritual wellbeing. In
the event you use any of the information in this book for yourself, which is your constitu-
tional right, the author and the publisher assume no responsibility for your actions.

A catalogue record for this book is available from the British Library.

ISBN 978-1-8485-0583-4

Printed and bound in Great Britain by TJ International, Padstow, Cornwall.

FSC
www.fsc.org
MIX
Paper from
responsible sources
FSC® C013056

One moment of total awareness is one moment of freedom and enlightenment.

—Manjusri, from "Song of the Wisdom-deity"

CONTENTS

Introduction: Making Peace with Time   1

Chapter 1   Awakening to Natural Time   15

Chapter 2   Taking Time for Your Higher Self   35

Chapter 3   Getting in Sync   61

Chapter 4   Understanding Our Powers of Perception   89

Chapter 5   Minding Time Wisely   111

Chapter 6   Creating Space in the Pace   135

Chapter 7   Living in Sacred Time and Space   157

Chapter 8   The Spinning Wheel of Time   181

            Conclusion: The Infinite Possibilities of Now   211

            Acknowledgments   215

            About Dzogchen Center   216

INTRODUCTION:
MAKING PEACE WITH TIME

To be able to be unhurried when hurried;
To be able not to slack off when relaxed;
To be able not to be frightened
And at a loss for what to do,
When frightened and at a loss;
This is the learning that returns us
To our natural state and transforms our lives.

—Liu Wenmin, early sixteenth-century poet

FOR EONS PEOPLE HAVE been grappling with the concept of time. From Sophocles to Ben Franklin to Einstein to Mick Jagger, the wisdom has been passed down to us: Time is the stuff life is made of. Time is money. Time is of the essence. Time flies. Time is relative. Time is on my side. Time is a cruel thief.

We measure time. We lose time. We kill time. We are strapped for time. These days, that last sentiment is what I hear most often from people. With varying degrees of vexation, agitation, or despair, they are constantly telling me, "I don't have enough time!"

It's not surprising that many of us feel this way. The pace of life today is far more frenetic than it was a generation ago, and unimaginably faster than what it was in the ancient world of Moses or Confucius. Trying to keep up with today's tempo can take a huge toll. That stress shows up in our suppressed immune systems, high blood pressure, heart attacks and stroke, insomnia, and digestive ailments. Stress contributes to the inability to think clearly or make competent decisions, to short tempers, and to sloppy work. As a result, we have more everyday problems: arguments at work and home, car accidents as we speed and yak on our cell phones, and unresolved grief because we don't have time to mourn properly. Stress also contributes to fertility problems, turns hair gray, and wears out bodies before their time. Long-term stress can even rewire the brain, leaving us more vulnerable to anxiety and depression, weight gain, and substance abuse.

I learned for myself some stark lessons about the daunting acceleration of life when I came back to the United States in the late 1980s after spending almost two decades in the East. I had lived in India and the Himalayas for most of my twenties, in a slow-paced, natural-rhythm, electricity-free zone. I then spent my early thirties in a traditional Tibetan *Dzogchen* meditation retreat at the Nyingma Retreat Center in the thickly forested Dordogne River valley of southern France. When I finally returned home I felt like Rip Van Winkle: The complexity of the world had increased so exponentially that modern American life was almost unrecognizable to me. I wasn't used to the rampant commercialism, the constant clamor of products being hawked. Even meditation centers and ashrams had become veritable spiritual supermarkets, with boutiques and cafés selling imported goods and wares to help support their nonprofit status.

As I began to adjust to a Western lifestyle after so long in monastic simplicity, what struck me more than anything else was the new aversion to the mundane tasks of daily life. Thus the ubiquitous time-saving tools—instant coffee, fast food, ATMs, microwave ovens, personal computers—as if somehow life would be better if we could speed our way through it. That message has only escalated since then. These days, young people tell me that they don't even have time for cell-phone conversations or e-mails. They prefer to text. The instant response that new technology allows has altered our perception of time. And ironically, most of us seem to feel we have far less time as a result.

Many of us feel that the modern efforts to save time have backfired, bringing onerous new problems of their own. Our technological advances and constant availability have blurred the line between leisure time and work. No sooner do we wrap our minds around a new computer program than it becomes obsolete. We can end up wasting precious minutes stuck on the phone with someone on the other side of the world, trying to figure out how to reset the computer brain in our dryer, or stove, or espresso machine. It takes time to learn how to do online banking, connect with friends on Facebook, master the complexities of smartphones and GPS units, and download a best seller to our e-readers. When Excel crashes and the work is lost after we've spent an hour entering data for a deadline, our blood pressure skyrockets. There's even technology to fix the stress created by technology. I recently learned of an experimental Google feature called Email Addict that shuts you out of your inbox, forcing compulsive e-mail checkers to give it a break.

Don't get me wrong. I think we're living in an amazing age, as miraculous and futuristic as anything out of the *Star Trek* and *Jetsons* episodes of my youth. I love being able to talk on my laptop face-to-face with someone on the other side of the world or to download a book or piece of music in a minute. The problem for a lot of us is figuring out how to disconnect from all this intensity for some peace and quiet. And how much of the time-related stress in our lives comes from trying to accommodate every single person who wants a piece of our day? Do you suffer from the "disease to please," striving to satisfy all those who make a claim on your time? Many of us are torn between the desire to be generous with our time and the need to conserve our own energy. It takes only a few seconds to read a 140-character Twitter message, but the cost of the total distraction lasts far longer. The thinner we spread ourselves, the more we skitter over the surface of our lives, never going deep. And since we can be tracked down just about anywhere, anytime, it seems there is literally no escape.

In the pages that follow, I'll teach you how to wean yourself from the addictions that sap time and energy, to clear out all the debris and distraction—in much the same way that a snow globe becomes calm and clear when you stop shaking it and allow the flakes to settle. You'll see, for example, that we can stay at our desks or in a traffic jam and, however momentarily, genuinely give our attention to the present moment as a way of finding inner peace.

I want to show you how to coexist peacefully with the inevitable, inexorable march of time. As a Buddhist, I've long studied the question of how to live authentically and joyfully in the present moment, and how to remain mindful, centered, and harmonious no matter what challenges come my way.

In a way, Buddhism is a profound study in time and time management, because the better you manage your mind and spirit, the less hold time has on you. Every moment can be lived fully, free and unconditioned, and every moment holds infinite possibilities and opportunities for a fresh start. Every moment of heightened consciousness is precious beyond price, for awareness is the primary currency of the human condition. Buddhism for me is a study in how to live fully and authentically, not only in our earthly time zone, but in what I call *Buddha Standard Time*—the dimension of timeless time, wholly *now*.

In recent years, I've had so many people ask me for help with finding their spiritual center in their out-of-control lives that I decided to make it the topic of this book—to show how we can discover a more calm, vibrant, and gratifying way of life. We can become masters rather than victims of a packed schedule and constant change, and feel composed in any situation—neither rushed nor overwhelmed, but peacefully in the moment. We can learn to set our own pace, a pace that makes sense in relation to who we are and what we need for our life journey.

One of the main obstacles to making peace with time is that we tend to experience it linearly: we keep moving forward, doing and accomplishing things, rather than just being. We are human *beings,* after all, not human *doings.* It costs us dearly to live only on the linear axis of time. We lose connection with our deeper and most authentic selves, too often mistaking mere movement for purpose and meaning. We adapt to a faster and faster tempo that keeps us feeling busy, but rarely with a sense of accomplishment. Staggering forward on a treadmill of events, we gather momentum until we lose any sense of how to stop. We are expert adapters, but the complexity and speed of our world require something other than merely adapting to its pace.

If we cultivate clarity, detachment, and equanimity, we can learn to remain still and calm amid the torrent of commitments, no longer allowing our overscheduled lives to rob us of the time we need to recalibrate and connect to the natural world, ourselves, and each other. For time moves on whether we are hurtling through life or savoring it. The big transformations can take place outside our daily awareness, until a stark reminder catches us up: hearing the new crack in the voice of a teenage son, perhaps, or seeing the unwelcome surprise of a gray hair, or wondering how it "suddenly" became winter.

We've also lost so much of our connection with the natural world that it doesn't seem to matter to many of us whether it's day or night, hot or cold, summer or winter. We control the climate at home, in the car, at the office, in the mall. We watch ball games at night under powerful lights. We eat food with little regard for season or source. These artificial means keep the rhythms and cycles of nature from us, further removing us from indicators of time passing. As we use up our limited natural resources, watch the ozone layer thin and glaciers melt, and hear about the extinction of species after species, it seems that the earth itself is gravely impermanent, a victim of time and change as surely as we all are.

We all experience time differently, depending on our frame of mind. When I returned home to Long Island for a visit after my first few years in India, I encountered not only a culture clash but a time clash with my parents. My mother didn't want me to meditate. Good Jewish mother that she was, she was fine if I napped every afternoon, but she felt that meditating was a waste of time—time that she felt I could have been spending with her and my father.

She was absolutely right in one sense: she hadn't seen her eldest son in years, and shutting myself in my room or wandering off into the backyard to meditate deprived us of precious hours together. But I had experienced another reality, a different way of being. I had learned that a meditation practice and a dedicated spiritual life lend time an infinitely expansive quality that would enhance every moment I spent with my parents. I knew that time need not be an either/or commodity, and that we always have the possibility of breaking out of linear time into a deeper dimension. When I rejoined my parents after an hour or two spent tapping into the timeless, I was a happier, more present, more patient, more aware, more engaged human being.

Right now you may still be struggling within the limited perspective of experiencing time linearly. "I can't do two things at once," you may find yourself saying. "There are only twenty-four hours in a day!" Even spiritual seekers wonder how they can possibly find enough time to meditate, study, chant, and pray. Our lives are crammed. Our calendars are full. It seems that something's got to give to allow time for the spiritual development that would allow us to break out of the linear lock. But that's not how it works. We don't need to find that impossible extra pocket of time in the day; rather, we can incorporate the spacious outlook of our spirituality into every minute of our life by reimagining and reframing the expanse of time we have.

Twenty-five hundred years ago, Buddha said that if we directly perceived the actual difficulties and sorrows of life, we'd practice to achieve enlightenment "as if our hair was on fire." A simple definition of enlightenment is the deep flash of awakening to the knowledge that we are much more than our time- and space-bound, material selves living in a material world. Some people awaken to enlightenment by grace, seemingly without effort, but most of us stay obsessively stuck in the past or the future, running our mental trains backward and forward on that track every minute of the day. We have a limited view of ourselves and our capacities. And nothing will change unless we stop the train and get off.

Emaho! (That's Tibetan for "Hallelujah!") We *can* stop the train. Buddhist wisdom teaches that the minutes and hours of our days do not merely march from future to present to past—looming, engulfing us, passing us by forever. Rather, each moment is intersected by a realm of infinite spaciousness and timelessness, known in Tibetan as *shicha,* the Eternal Now. This is the precious awakened dimension that I call Buddha Standard Time, and it is available to us every instant.

"Let go the past," the Buddha said, "let go the future, and let go what is in between, transcending the things of time. With your mind free in every direction, you will not return to birth and aging." When we are in touch with being only in the present moment, only with *what is,* instead of what we regret, fear, or anticipate, our sense of limits in time will no longer have negative power over our lives. This is ancient, timeless wisdom. People have been writing about living in the present moment as far back as the Pharaoh Akhenaton, who in the fourteenth century BCE wrote, "He who neglects the present moment throws away all he has."

This is something we all need to remember every day. We can't afford to wait to learn that lesson. "It's now or never, as always," I like to say. Be present in this moment, as if it's the only moment. This breath, as if it's the only breath. That is how we meditate, lead mindful and centered lives, and stay in the now. And that is how we begin to make peace with time and with ourselves.

In Buddha Standard Time, there are no small-minded contortions over a mentally constructed world. It is a place of being, not doing, a much vaster dimension than the one most of us habitually inhabit. I will show you how to get out of your frenzied time zone and into that timeless dimension, no matter where you are or what you are doing. There you will feel balanced, clear, joyful, and able to function at your best.

When you learn to live in Buddha Standard Time, bringing what I call *nowness-awareness* into your daily life, you'll be more present and engaged in your interactions. You'll be better able to negotiate the rough patches, sensing when to assert yourself and when to withdraw. Above all, you won't fear that life will pass you and your loved ones by, but will recognize that we each have our own pace and way of blooming. You'll feel clear about your ability to discover happiness and fulfillment. Nowness-awareness is the secret of enlightenment and self-realization: the Buddha within.

You'll see that living in Buddha Standard Time is in no way antithetical to modern life but gives you the tools to live it sanely and joyfully. Neither planning ahead nor reminiscing about the past need obscure the clarity of our present awareness. The Buddha would say: If you're planning ahead, just plan ahead. If you're remembering, just remember. We can look forward or back without fretting or obsessing, or allowing concerns about the future to constrict freedom in the present. Think about it: even contemplating the future or the past is a function of present awareness.

We can always choose how to respond, what to do, how to live. We always have time to take a breath and begin again, revitalized, awake, aware.

When we understand and connect with our true, timeless natures, we will automatically slow down. And when we slow down, time slows down as well, so we perceive that we have more of it. The more aware we are and the more quickly our minds process things, the slower they seem to occur—just as time seems to slow down on that first glorious autumn morning, when the colors and the breeze come alive under our intensely focused attention.

We can learn to experience a similar heightened awareness every day. We then have more room to choose, reflect, attend, respond intentionally, and thus make the most of our time and the opportunities given us by this magical life. We can learn to do things sensibly and sequentially when we're under pressure, turning off the harried mental chatter that makes us feel we must do several things at once.

The more conscious we become of our key stressors and the unproductive habits we've developed around time, the closer we'll be to freeing ourselves from their net. A skillful relationship with the pace of life on this earth means that every choice, every action, and every breath can be whole and complete. We can be fully, vibrantly present. This is the secret, hidden in plain sight if only we open our eyes to see it.

Whether you're a Buddhist or not, this book will give you the inspiration and tools to reduce the amount of stress in your life and help you find more focus, fulfillment, creativity, and wisdom. I'll show you how to integrate mini–stress busters into your day, the simple meditative pause that can fit in anywhere, and how to enrich your daily life with true awakefulness. There's no rule that meditation must be done sitting cross-legged on a cushion. As you'll see, we can practice meditation on a nature walk or even while washing the dishes. In the beginning, you will learn how to pick up and carry awareness practice with you wherever you go; later, stable mindfulness gently empowers and carries you. This is the blessing of a genuine spiritual path.

Each chapter has one "Mindful Moments" exercise and one "Time Out" meditation. The former offers advice and practices to incorporate into your day to begin to transform your old relationship with time. And the latter provides a calming, meditative pause. I'll show how to incorporate practices from other spiritual traditions as well—the Jewish Sabbath being a classic example, or a pilgrimage like the one Muslims make to Mecca—to help you slow down, be present, and embrace time's infinite possibilities.

With practice you'll find that taking time to meditate will actually save you time and enable you to do more. It will increase your energy, alertness, and stamina in the same way that athletes who do their calisthenics every day keep in optimal shape to improve their performance and face challenges. I offer an eclectic mix of techniques for meditating and living in the now, drawn from Tibetan Buddhist tradition as well as from other great wisdom traditions, neuroscientific research, and holistic mind–body approaches.

Buddha's ancient prescription for enlightened living is scientific in that it can, like a science experiment, be replicated. Anyone who follows the principles of mindfulness will come into harmony and balance with the natural world and progressively realize his or her innate spiritual nature, a nature that is not fixed in time. This is the enlightened Buddha's primordial promise, and millions have achieved it.

The following chapters cover the essential aspects of making peace with time, living in the moment, and realizing our potential. As you read through them, you will learn to synchronize with the rhythms and cycles of nature, including your own mind and body, cells and tissues, and neural pathways. You will learn how to slow down or accelerate time, to have richer relationships, a more productive work life, and much less stress. Ultimately, you will arrive at the shore of the boundless, universal, and everlasting, and know that it has been with you every moment along the way.

Each time you repeat a "Time Out" meditation, it will take you more deeply into the moment, and each time you repeat a "Mindful Moments" exercise, you will learn something new. As Goldilocks might explain, your first reading of a suggested meditation or exercise will invariably be too broad, your second reading will be too narrow, and your third reading will be just right! In Buddhism, this is known as the Middle Way—a moderate, balanced, and flexible path of life.

The focus of the chapters is as follows:

1. AWAKENING TO NATURAL TIME. In the first chapter, you will learn how to awaken from the tyranny of artificial modern time. You will rediscover the multiple cycles of growth, change, and decay in the natural world around you and learn a mini-meditation or "breath break" to refresh yourself, increase your attentiveness, and strengthen your resolve throughout the day.

2. TAKING TIME FOR YOUR HIGHER SELF. In the second chapter, you will learn how to take time for your higher Self—your noblest, deepest nature—in contrast to the small, separate self whose fleeting moods change from second to second, day to day, and year to year. You will begin to feel less time pressured and distracted and see time as your ally and friend rather than as an enemy or tormenter.

3. GETTING IN SYNC. In the third chapter, you will learn to go deeper into the flow of life and learn to synchronize linear Father Time and cyclical Mother Nature (manifested, for example, in left-brain and right-brain thinking, respectively); attune to the natural circadian rhythms of your body as well as your meridians and chakras, or natural energy centers; and give voice to your innermost heartbeat, the most reliable timepiece you have.

4. UNDERSTANDING OUR POWERS OF PERCEPTION. This chapter examines the phenomenon of time being in the mind, and the gifts of perception—our own and that of others. From bodhisattvas or angels around us who provide exactly what we need just when we need it, to what appears as psychic ability, to compassion and loving-kindness, to aging as a state of mind, you will learn how mindful awareness brings to fruition our phenomenal ability to perceive and connect.

5. MINDING TIME WISELY. In the fifth chapter, you will learn to practice the contemplative arts of mindfulness and presencing, which is meditation in action. You will learn to go more deeply into the moment to experience its richness, subtlety, and promise.

6. CREATING SPACE IN THE PACE. In the sixth chapter, you will begin to master living in the moment by expanding and contracting time according to your personal needs and desires, as well as varying the tempo.

7. LIVING IN SACRED TIME AND SPACE. In the seventh chapter, you will learn how to create or fashion temporal and spatial refuges—the foundation for putting forth your best efforts and realizing your life's full potential. You will learn how to engage and synchronize better with others and find meaningful personal and social outlets for your skills, talents, and creative energy.

8. THE SPINNING WHEEL OF TIME. In this chapter, you will learn to experience sickness, loss, death, and other ravages of time as natural aspects of life, to be gracefully embraced in their seasons, rather than as untimely interruptions, threats, and enemies, and you will consider the global aspects of time. Finally, you will learn to balance and synchronize all the temporal dimensions to enter Buddha Standard Time and become one with the radiant, timeless ground of your being.

As you progress through the book, you will find your notions of time and self undergoing a change. You will evolve from darkness to light, from confusion to wisdom, from selfishness to unselfishness, from a separate self to your divine Buddha nature. This is the promise and premise of the spiritual path, the miracle of genuine awakefulness.

In Buddha Standard Time you will come to realize that, in spite of your hectic days, you have much more time than you think. In fact, you have all the time in the world.

Awakening to Natural Time

ROSALIND. I pray you, what is't o'clock?
ORLANDO. You should ask me what time o' day; there's no clock in the forest.

—Shakespeare, *As You Like It*

FROM SWITZERLAND—THE BEAUTIFUL, NEUTRAL land of high Alpine mountains, pristine lakes, and charming handicrafts—comes this bizarre story:

The clockmaster A. P. Simmerling yesterday wrecked his own business, causing damages of two hundred thousand dollars to his clocks. According to insiders, Mr. Simmerling was a perfectionist, and he always tried to synchronize all the clocks in his shop. The introduction of summer and wintertime, in which all the clocks had to be periodically set backwards or forwards, proved to be too much of a challenge to bridge. It became Mr. Simmerling's self-appointed mission to smash the entire interior of his shop with a pre-war German cuckoo clock. Miraculously, the little birdie survived the massacre. Until at least an hour after the carnage, a Frisian standing clock also continued crying for help. Luckily, there was a funny farm nearby where not only the patients but the clocks ran late. After all the clocks were silenced and her husband was led away, Mrs. Simmerling confided to local authorities of a great relief.

An obsession with order and time can drive us mad. Clocks, like modern society, are impersonal and mechanical, and sometimes they make us want to rebel. Although most of us will not wind up smashing our clocks to pieces like poor Mr. Simmerling, the first step toward living in Buddha Standard Time is learning to release ourselves from the tyranny of artificial time. When we harmonize with nature and the rhythmic flow of Natural Time, we rediscover the cycles of growth, change, decay, and regeneration in the world around us, bringing a better sense of awareness and connectedness to our busy days.

Since the earliest humans learned to tell the days, months, and years by observing the heavens, we have been imposing order on the flow of time. Calendars, zodiacs, and other inventions helped us calculate the rising and setting of the sun and moon and connect the dots between the stars and our earthly fortunes. The Egyptians invented the sundial and water clock, the first timepieces, contributing to the orderly functioning of early civilization. The Chinese gave us the sextant, allowing nautical timing and measurement by the motions of the stars and the celestial clock. The Indians conceived the *kalpa,* an immeasurably long eon, beautifully defined as the time it takes a rare Himalayan bird to, stroke by stroke, wear down Mt. Sumeru with the brush of a silk scarf in its beak. The Maya, the greatest timekeepers of antiquity, left behind seventeen calendars, including the Long Count, which runs out in 2012. The Incas kept time upon intricately knotted strings, some of which survive. The Romans gave us the Julian calendar and leap year. The British bequeathed the time zones and Greenwich mean time, the Swiss the cuckoo clock and bejeweled watch, and the Americans the atomic clock and the big bang, the theoretical start of it all.

Until the Renaissance, humans operated mostly on Natural Time—in sync with the daylight and darkness, the seasons, the tides, and other terrestrial and celestial cycles. But in perhaps the greatest time innovation of all, with the Industrial Revolution, not only were handicrafts displaced by more efficiently manufactured goods, but time itself became a commodity—and an increasingly scarce and valuable one at that. The world has been shrinking and spinning faster and faster ever since, as everyone works harder to produce more in less time.

Starbucks recently shaved eight seconds off the wait time at its counters by waiving signatures on all credit-card orders of less than twenty-five dollars. It saved another fourteen seconds by introducing a larger scoop so that baristas need to dip into the ice bucket only once to make a large Frappuccino. If you are waiting in a long line, as I have, for your early-morning pick-me-up, you appreciate the minutes saved. But multiply this breakneck example many times over and it becomes clear that we're growing accustomed to a lightning-fast lifestyle that ultimately puts stress on us all.

From early morning to late at night, from preschool to retirement, responsible citizens that we are, we rush through our lives in order to scrimp on time. But what if time did not control us? What if we felt that our time and our lives were our own? The first step toward reclaiming them is to awaken to Natural Time, to get back in touch with the rhythms that humans observed until just a couple of centuries ago, and that some traditional societies in undeveloped countries still observe. Those clans, tribes, and nomads may be trying to modernize and progress both materially and technologically, but we have much to learn by getting back in touch with their respect for the timeless and primordial rhythms of Natural Time.

Buddhist Time Management

I think I've been studying time my whole life, but looking back, I see I was not always connected to Natural Time. As a kid living in suburban Long Island with a restless spirit mostly channeled through a love of competitive sports, I grew up tethered to the clock and stopwatch. By age twenty, though, I was thousands of miles away, in dusty, windswept Rajasthan, India, where I sat in silent meditation for ten days in a Buddhist shrine hall. Always a bit of a control freak with an inborn sense of responsibility not to waste a single hour, minute, or second, I suddenly had to surrender to days divided into twelve- to fourteen-hour-long meditation sessions, punctuated only by temple chimes; hours spent in total silence except for periods of chanting and one fifty-minute Buddhist discourse from the meditation master each evening. To my initial dismay, there were no meals after midday. But there was plenty of time to ruminate from noon till breakfast the next morning. In that extraordinary environment, I heard and experienced what Buddha said: to enjoy good health, to bring true happiness to one's family, to bring peace to all, one must first discipline and refine one's mind.

As for myself, I was sitting there partly because of the turmoil back home. The '60s had turned the world upside down. With bombs falling on rice farmers in Vietnam and peaceful Buddhist monks setting themselves on fire—my first image of Buddhism—I didn't know any longer how to live my life. So after college I gathered together money I'd received as graduation gifts and money I'd saved from my bar mitzvah and summer jobs, sold my guitar, my typewriter, and my textbooks, and got on a plane to India. My brain was whirling with questions. In that topsy-turvy era when four young working-class rockers from England were the world's highest authorities on love, peace, and the meaning of life, authentic answers were in short supply. I didn't realize yet that I had come to India, following in the footsteps of the Beatles, to learn about time, spaciousness, and eternity.

I had traveled not only five thousand miles across the globe but also a century or two backward, to a forgotten world. First I lived in India, a Third World country on the cusp of modernity, then ended up in the Himalayan world of medieval Tibet and Tibetan Buddhism. The ashrams and monasteries I studied in over the next twenty-five years were still operating according to centuries-old Tibetan Buddhist traditions, without newspapers, telecommunications, central heating, and in some cases even electricity or plumbing. Yet those of us who lived in joyous fellowship there, studying and practicing the Great Way of Awakening, felt grateful and serene, and rich in an abundance of innate resources. Nor did our simple quality of life seem temporary or merely preparatory, but complete and sufficient unto itself.

At first, the hour-long meditation sessions, the afternoon-long lectures, and the chanted ritual liturgies seemed interminable. But after a while I stopped marking how the day moved ahead—the hours, minutes, and yes, even seconds on my watch. The more settled and concentrated my mind became, forty-five minutes, an hour, an afternoon would go by imperceptibly. Then, several days would vanish without a trace. I learned to observe the inhalations and exhalations of my breath, and focus only there—in the immediacy and freshness of the now—while letting everything else come and go. Breathing in and out, and becoming simply aware of it. Watching the breath . . . becoming the breath . . . being the breath. No time, no space or location. Nothing needing to be done. No one trying to get anywhere. What peace, what harmony, what bliss.

The more I practiced meditation, the better I got, until one day I sensed myself *outside of time*. Everything was perfectly at rest and in complete harmony, just as it was. After that fleeting yet unforgettable breakthrough experience, it became a little easier for me to meditate, but it would take a long time to unwind the superficial complexities and conditioning of my former self. Eventually I learned how to just sit, breathe, and be—present, lucid, and aware. Transparent to myself. Seeing Buddha, Being Buddha became my motto. Sitting still, slowing down, taking the time to breathe and observe my surroundings—in short, meditation—was the key to awakening myself to Natural Time.

Through countless hours of meditation, I uncovered a secret: *the more concentration and awareness I managed to achieve, the more time disappeared.* It's not *time* that we lack in our rushed lives, but *focus.* The more we slow down our speedy, obsessive thought process and sustain mindful awareness, the better listeners and friends, mates and coworkers we become, and the more clarity, serenity, centeredness, and direct immediacy of experience we discover within ourselves. We have more time to evaluate and respond intelligently to things rather than just blindly reacting. Clearer forks emerge in our path. Heightened awareness sharpens and nourishes us, and renders us fully capable of embracing life rather than feeling overwhelmed by it.

Over the following years, I continued to feel the benefits of Buddhist mindfulness meditation through numerous retreats and regular daily practice, and ultimately made a momentous decision. I would commit to a long, *very* long, cloistered retreat in southern France to be trained as a lama—a Tibetan Buddhist teacher, meditation master, and spiritual guide. As prescribed by Tibetan tradition, the training period would last three years, three months, and three days. During these eleven hundred days, the entire energy system—including chakras and internal energies as well as spiritual consciousness—is entirely regenerated and revitalized.

I was scared by the prospect. But as it turned out, it was similar to my earlier experiences in the Indian desert: the first year stretched out a bit, the second year went faster, and by the third year I no longer wondered which day, which month, how long; I wasn't constrained by concepts of past and future. I was, at last, able to be intensely present in each moment. The eight subsequent years I spent at that forest cloister passed swiftly in a peaceful flow.

All of those experiences changed me and taught me that time is mainly in the mind. When we stop our minds, even for a moment, we stop the universe: no time, no space, no conditioning and compulsions. Just limitless peace and harmony. In Zen, this "taste" of enlightenment, fleeting yet timeless, is known as *satori* (breakthrough). It is a momentary illumination, the sudden appearance of a bright star on the horizon or in your heart that will guide you the rest of your days. By following the lessons in this book, beginning with awakening to Natural Time, you will, I hope, experience satori, too.

Buddha's Timeless Teaching

According to legend, King Suddhodana, Prince Siddhartha's father, groomed his son to become a great warrior and succeed him as the ruler of a mighty state in what is now Nepal. To steel his will in the face of life's tribulations and keep him from both temptation and existential reflection, the king protected his son from all sorrows, sufferings, social ills, and iniquities—in short, all the ravages of time. However, one day young Siddhartha strayed from the palace grounds and encountered an elderly man who was toothless and blind. The cloistered prince had never seen anyone like this before and was stunned to realize that despite his wealth, power, and knowledge, someday he, too, would age and suffer. Then he encountered in succession a feverish, tormented man lying sick on the ground with the plague, a corpse being cremated as tearful family and friends wept and mourned, and a peacefully smiling monk in orange robes with a shaved head.

Dazed, depressed, stimulated, and even exhilarated at his discovery of old age, sickness, death, and the spiritual life, Siddhartha returned to the palace and its facade of eternal splendor and beauty to discover that his adoring young wife had given birth to their baby. Rather than being over-joyed, the prince felt terror-stricken at the thought of what lay ahead for his son. He now knew that time's scythe would ultimately cut everyone down. Instead of taking his place as master of the household, completing his martial-arts training, and preparing to wield the scepter of his earthly kingdom, Siddhartha escaped from the palace so he could follow the path of the peaceful monk and find deathless truth and eternal fulfillment— what he termed "the heart's sure release." In a word, enlightenment.

Siddhartha went through many trials and austerities, veering close to death more than once, and eventually came to terms with this now glori-ous, now horrifying, but always transitory and ephemeral thing we call life. After his enlightenment, he reconciled with his family and taught his mother and son as well as countless others the secrets of timeless living.

Siddhartha came in contact with illness, aging, death, and the spiri-tual life, which are known as the Four Sights. They constitute the essence of the spiritual path—recognizing impermanence, coming to terms with it, and overcoming the suffering it causes. Although Buddhism is widely appreciated for its ethical teachings and attitude-transforming tech-niques, at its heart is a profound insight into the nature of time and how to master it.

Siddhartha became known as the Buddha, or Awakened One. For forty-five years he taught tirelessly throughout India, showing people how to realize their original goodness and inherent wisdom: free, infinite, incor-ruptible true essence, or what later followers came to call *innate Buddha-nature*. He showed them how to overcome the suffering and dysfunction caused by their insatiable cravings and difficulty dealing with change and time. He taught us that *we suffer because of our denial of and resistance to time's flow, and our clinging to illusions of fixity and security.*

Rediscovering Nature's Rhythms

Most of us have a hard time letting these notions fall from our grasp. We can't get outside of time to be able to master it. No matter what we do, we are surrounded by ceaseless change. The grass and flowers grow in the balmy warmth of spring, the foliage reaches a peak in the intense heat of summer, the leaves fall in the cool autumn, and life grows quiescent in the cold and ice of winter. Then after the snow melts and the ground thaws, the cycle begins anew.

We experience growth, change, and decay in countless natural cycles throughout the day, the year, and from birth to death. We experience how our consciousness changes as we grow and develop, and how much our thoughts and feelings, perceptions and opinions, change, too, year by year and even moment to moment. We can notice that the sea has ground the rocky shoreline to sand—without necessarily perceiving the slow but certain progress—and that the wind has bent a tree until it points leeward. Even the hard, tall standing stones from megalithic times, the Great Pyramid of Giza, and our own steel-encased skyscrapers are caught up in the flow of inexorable change and impermanence.

Although you may have heard it said that time is an illusion in some ultimate sense, on the biological level of aging and death, time is real enough. It inexorably proceeds apace in a series of events, from fleeting internal mind moments to external clock times. We have simply lost touch with time's natural expression.

There is a Native American prayer from the Ojibwa that goes: "O Grandfather, Sacred One, teach us love, compassion, and honor, that we may heal the earth and heal each other." Communing with the spirit of nature is the oldest form of religious worship throughout the world, and for good reason. The early American naturalist John Muir wrote, "When one tugs at a single thing in nature, he finds it attached to the rest of the world."

In my lectures, I always advise people to spend some time outdoors every day, even if only taking one deep breath out of the window or stargazing on their way to their front door. Do the same, and you will find that nature's rhythm will begin to tug on you. It's not difficult to find times throughout the year when natural cycles provide an impulse to stop and remember that life consists of more than making a living. Most of us feel giddy in spring, as the sap rises and the day lengthens. Perhaps we are intellectually invigorated, as well as somewhat wistful, in the fall as the leaves turn and the light lessens. Nature invites us in all of her many forms to look deeper at such times.

When was the last time you felt the supportive, accepting vital energy of our earthly mother? Was it when you were a child, lying on your back in the grass? Or on a beach, with the distant sound of the surf? Barefoot in your garden, perhaps, with the feeling of tingling warmth coming up from the soil?

A study of biophilia (love of the living world) done by hospital designer Barbara Huelat showed that nature, in some respects, is equal to yoga, exercise, and meditation in its ability to relieve stress. A study done on people recovering from surgery in a major hospital showed that those patients who were able to look out of a window at flowers, trees, or the sky during their healing process recovered more quickly and with less pain than those who had no view to the outdoors.

Nature is the original fountain of knowledge, beauty, sustenance, and spiritual inspiration for all people everywhere. She belongs to no one and to everyone. Like our ancestors, we can learn to cherish her just as she embraces and holds us. In Tibetan Buddhism we call the intrinsic magic of reality *drala*—this beyondness that is available through each moment. We can call upon *drala* as an ally, as a way to reach beyond ourselves, when we need to take refuge from confusion and distress and find respite from the storm and stress of daily life. It is a way of accessing the invisible, the form-less, the subtler dimensions of energy and reality.

We also can simply recognize *drala* through those moments when we are moved and pulled out of ourselves almost accidentally, by whatever most transports us and reconnects to what is beyond, yet simultaneously within, each of us. As children, we used to lie in the grass and stare up at the clouds and the sky, losing ourselves, forgetting ourselves—looking at the spacious sky, becoming spacious and skylike, being one with the sky, whether consciously or not. As adults we look at the ocean's waves, listen to a waterfall, or stare at a candle flame, a fire in the hearth, or a bonfire. The natural elemental energy of water and fire transports us far beyond our limited selves.

This is living in Natural Time. It is not at all foreign to us. These are the simple, practical essentials of natural mysticism. Reunion with the natural state is the meaning of the word *yoga* (whose literal meaning is "union with god" and which is derived from the Sanskrit word meaning "yoke").

So, how can we reach and sustain that state that we knew as children and now enter into only sporadically? Many of us have learned to tran-scend ordinary time and be transported into a splendid higher reality through prayer or contemplation in a church, temple, mosque, or place of pilgrimage. But what loftier, more moving cathedral is there than a red-wood forest or a massive mountain range? Or what shrine or sanctuary more uplifting to the soul than watching a vast, shimmering desert, a calm sylvan lake in summer, or a radiant sunset over the ocean?

Reflect on the most sublime moments in your life, and recall how many of them were in serene, natural settings like these. Then see if you can re-create that feeling or image in your mind's eye, if just for a few sec-onds. And then when you get a chance, go outdoors and find a quiet place to experience that moment of grace. It is a choice to go through life with a cell phone in your hand. Disconnect yourself from the wondrous gifts of our technology often enough to remember that natural wonders have always existed and have always brought solace.

For most of human existence, the sky was our only calendar. A human being innately feels at home in nature. We enjoy walking on the earth, flexing our mental and physical muscles, and can tell the time of day by a glance at the sun or moon. We are in touch with the rising and falling tides, like our own internal rhythms; the waxing and waning of our mate's or child's life energy as well as our own; and the lunar monthly cycles, solstices and equinoxes, bright harvest moons, and local festivals, feasts, and celebrations. We know how to let go without letting go too late or too soon. As you enter more fully into Buddha Standard Time in the chapters that follow, you will feel more in sync with nature and the multiple cycles around you.

TIME OUT

Rediscover the Sky

As kids, most of us experienced *drala* in looking up at the sky, finding shapes in the clouds or staring in wonderment at the stars at night, perhaps learning to name some constellations. A simple way to reconnect with the magic and profundity of Natural Time is to do as you did as a child.

Go out at night, lie on your back, and look up at the stars. Take a few deep breaths while you raise your gaze and experience the immensity of the sky. See individual stars, clusters of stars, and the entire panoramic sweep of sky overhead. If friends will be joining you, tell them in advance that you and they won't be talking during this time but communing together in another way.

Focus both your gaze and your awareness on the infinite sky, breathe out into the yawning heavens, and relax. Rest at ease, awake and aware.

Let the air, the wind, and the sky flow in and out through you and fill you with light and space. Be calm and clear, at home and at ease.

Observe.

Allow. Accept.

Embrace and surrender.

Letting go means letting come and go,

letting be.

This is the secret essence of inner freedom and autonomy:

Letting be.

Be still.

All is right here;

Don't stray elsewhere.

If you've never meditated before . . . now you have. Well done!

I was once talking with my neighbor Peter, a partner in a high-powered law firm, about my morning ritual of meditating by a stone Buddha in my garden. Peter shook his head sadly and said, "I wish I had time to do that. It feels like I barely have enough time to brush my teeth in the morning, before rushing to catch the six A.M. train." Peter explained how after a power breakfast with his associates, he litigated on behalf of his clients, clocking every billable minute throughout the day, and typically got home just in time to say goodnight to his wife and kids. "I am crazy busy every single day. I think it's giving me an ulcer. Is there a mantra you can give me to help calm me down?" he asked.

Of course there are many chants I could have shared with Peter. But more than a mantra, he needed a simple meditation to get him back in sync with nature. I told him he needed to observe the sunrise and sunset for a few minutes each day, coordinating his routine with the daily rising and setting of the sun. He looked dubious but said he'd give it a try.

The next time I saw Peter, a month later, he smiled and waved to me as he jogged across the street to chat. "I can't believe how glorious the sunrise is," he marveled. "And the sunset! There's a different array of colors every night. I thought I would find this a chore to squeeze into my day, but I can't tell you how good it made me feel! I've begun to focus better at work, and you know what? I'm starting to feel like I have *more* time, not less."

It's amazing how such a simple exercise, perhaps taking only five or ten minutes each morning and evening, can transform a person's entire mood and outlook on life. Reconnecting with nature enabled Peter to release some of the anxiety of his busy life. As we shall see in the pages that follow, moments like these allow us to start reprogramming our neural pathways. And from the larger celestial view, taking in the sun's energy also produces an effect in which micro- and macrocosm unite for several precious moments of timelessness. With a minor adjustment to his day, Peter achieved enormous benefits.

This priceless experience was absolutely free. (No, I didn't charge him for the advice.) An amazing orchestra of life, death, and rebirth is playing all around us. We need only take the time to observe and listen. By returning to Natural Time and freeing ourselves from our watches, schedules, and deadlines, we will find that everything begins to unfold more smoothly.

When you are in a good frame of mind, take off your watch. And put away your cell phone and other electronic devices. Take a walk, take a nap, or sit or lie in a bathtub, pool, lake, or hammock, with no time referents of any kind.

Relax and enter into a timeless zone: nowhere to go, nothing to do, free of scheduling and appointments, free of past and future thoughts and memories and plans. Simply and attentively present, you are cultivating nowness-awareness.

You can also try removing your watch in your everyday routine. At the office, in the supermarket, out with friends . . . you may be surprised at the new, expansive relationship you have with time when you stop measuring it in small increments.

The primacy of the moment is one of the first things you discover when you get off artificial clock time. It's always now. Not earlier, not later, not yesterday, not tomorrow, but right now. Your focus is no longer on your schedule—where you have to be and what you have to do—but in the present. When you think about it, the present moment is the one and only place we are or ever can be. It holds infinite ways of knowing our greatness, our individual genius—infinite resources for solving problems. And we can experience the present moment wherever we are, whenever we choose, just by becoming precisely focused on the breath or on any other equally vibrant, ever-available object of attention.

This is the first lesson I learned in meditation in India and the one I would like to share with you: how to center yourself and to fully and completely invest this moment with your total attention, *as if it were your only moment.* For it is, in a manner of speaking. Recalling the past and planning for the future are activities that can happen only in the present. "The future is now," as we used to say in the '60s. When we learn how to make it a habit to stay focused in the now, time seems to disappear, and we are continually renewed, refreshed, energized, and free. Whether we are indoors or out, in the high Himalayas without another soul around or in Walmart during the Christmas rush, the moment is all we have.

"Breathe, Smile, Relax"

You can begin to incorporate the following simple awareness practice— "Breathe, Smile, Relax"—into your busy life right now. From the time Siddhartha sat under the leafy Bodhi Tree (the fig tree where he attained complete enlightenment) with the turquoise sky overhead, a rustling brook to one side, and golden rice fields stretching to the horizon, this exercise has been done in one form or another for more than twenty-five hundred years. The first "Mindful Moments" exercise of the book will help you awaken to Natural Time and its coursing pulses and cadences.

A Breath Break

Sitting still in a quiet place—ideally, outdoors in nature,
but indoors, if you like—
bring all of your attention to your body as you fill your lungs
with one deep, deep breath . . .
and then let it out in a long sigh. . . .

If you are truly attentive, your mind will be clear of all distractions for ten whole seconds, while your body is nourished with extra oxygen and your heart is touched with a little divine peace. Even with only one breath cycle, you may have felt a touch of serenity, a little loosening of your jaw, and an ability to think more clearly afterward. So simple, a trip into Natural Time!

Try it again. Three breaths or more might be needed, depending on your own self-awareness and inclination:

Breathe deep.
Smile.
Relax. . . .

James Joyce, the great novelist and master of Natural Time (whose *Finnegans Wake*—or Awakening—ends with the beginning of a sentence and begins with the end of the same sentence), called this state of suspended animation outside the passage of time "aesthetic arrest," a single moment of ecstasy. Your life will transform if you just begin to insert these little breath breaks or moments of attentiveness throughout your day. Try it!

The lesson is not to compartmentalize your life, with 99 percent spent in busyness and 1 percent in spiritual nourishment. Instead, train yourself to integrate this sublime awareness into each moment as an enlightening way of life and a path of joy.

Bringing focused attention to your breath in the ever-present moment is the most basic of all meditation practices and the first step to entering Natural Time. Try not to feel daunted by the idea of adding another commitment to the many you already have. Give it a chance. Consider the alternative: if during the course of an ordinary day, strapped for time as usual, you often find your mind racing, your heart pounding, and your shoulders hunched up around your ears, it's time to stop ignoring these signs. Turn off the air conditioner and open your car windows as you drive. Take off your shoes and walk barefoot in the grass. Listen to the birds. Breathe in and out the oxygen and other elements in the atmosphere that have animated countless amoebas and woolly mammoths and form the elemental building blocks of everything from stardust to supernovas.

Pets and wild animals live in Natural Time. And they are often attracted to the peaceful, loving feelings of meditation. I have a fond memory from decades ago of sitting in meditation very early one morning beneath a tree in the national forest on the slopes of stunning Mt. Shasta in California. Suddenly I felt a nibble through the cape around my shoulders. I opened my eyes to find myself peering into the peaceful, fearless eyes of a doe. We shared an indescribably beautiful moment of connection for what seemed an eternity before she turned and gently walked away into the forest.

Our true, intrinsic nature is free, open, flowing, and joyful, while at the same time clear, radiant, and centered. This is what we seek to liberate and actualize when we devote ourselves to awakening to Natural Time and beginning to live in the moment.

Scientists and medical doctors are now discovering the multiple benefits of meditation. In recent years, they have reported that regular meditation can lower blood pressure, reduce the risk of heart attack, stroke, and heart failure, decrease stress hormones like cortisol, and reduce inflammatory processes associated with atherosclerosis. They are also finding that meditation can help improve memory, awareness, attention, and other facets of time management. For example, in a recent study published in the online journal *PloS Biology*, researchers reported that three months of breathing exercises like the breath break can lead to a profound shift in how the brain allocates attention. And who doesn't have attention issues today, in our society that pulls our attention in a multitude of directions at once?

Studies by psychologists such as Michael McGee of Harvard Medical School have found that meditation benefits the brain by increasing gray matter, improving the immune function, reducing stress, and promoting a sense of balance, clarity, equanimity, and well-being.

Scientists used to assume that our attention span was relatively fixed. To their surprise, they discovered that attention is a flexible, trainable skill. The practical effect of meditation is to slow down time, focus attention, and increase alert nowness-awareness. It is an essential tool to help us manage our overscheduled lives.

I have often noticed that we Westerners seem to know only high gear or neutral. Many of us work hard all week and then totally flop on the weekend or on vacation. We're not too good when it comes to smoothly shifting to an in-between state and staying there. Cultivating awareness and appreciation of the present moment helps us feel more centered: we can keep our ship aright amid stormy seas and relax when the waters are calm, without extremes in either situation. It helps to learn to take the pressure off ourselves with our endless responsibilities and lists.

Ten years ago I was having dinner with Joseph Goldstein, an old friend and pioneering Western Buddhist Dharma teacher. We were discussing work and common friends in our extended spiritual family. During dessert, I was telling him what my late *Dzogchen* meditation master Nyoshul Khenpo Rinpoche had told me on his deathbed in Dordogne, France. I mentioned that, among other things, he had charged me with the mission of identifying one hundred disciples and Dharma-heirs (lineage successors). I told Joseph how that felt like a great endorsement from my enlightened master, yet also a huge challenge and an almost impossible feat. And Joseph told me what he had learned: you don't have to do it all right now, or even in this lifetime!

That felt like a huge relief. Ever since then, whenever I face a large task I say to myself, "Not all right now." Take the pressure off when you can by repeating the same words.

Silence

Meditating at home can really help you center and relax, but that might seem impossible at work when you're under the pressure of a deadline or other time-related stress. It may seem contradictory to say that relaxing requires conscious effort, yet it is the act of consciously noticing where you are—in a state of stress, for example—and then consciously deciding how you'd rather be that makes it happen. When you relax in meditation, it does help, of course, if you drop your shoulders, let go of the physical tension and mental preoccupations, and let your jaw loosen. But relaxation is not only about releasing tension from your physical body. "You've got to relax your mind," as the classic Leadbelly song goes. To relax is to let go, let be. If we're really relaxed, we're letting everything come and go—thoughts, feelings, worries, bodily tension; just watching it happen, not attaching to or identifying with any of it. Free from pushing and pulling, judging and evaluating, interference and manipulation.

You can learn to relax in even the most challenging environments. One of the best public speakers I've ever heard is Marian Wright Edelman, a lawyer, activist, and founder of the Children's Defense Fund. Busy as she is, and wherever she may be, each week Marian takes time to enjoy a day of silence. Once she was climbing in the Alps with some friends from Harvard. When her day of quiet came, she explained that she was going to keep silent, that the others were free to hike and climb with her but should not expect to hear her speak. When her friend Dick found Marian sitting on a big boulder near the top of a mountain pass on their arduous trek, he sat next to her for half an hour and enjoyed the view before they eventually joined up with the rest of their party. He later told me those moments of stillness with Marian were absolutely the best part of the journey and the only time he fully experienced the true splendor of the Alpine range.

You, too, can incorporate a period of Noble Silence (as this practice is known in Buddhism) into your life. Even amid the most hectic modern lifestyles, true serenity can be found by silently reconnecting with a tree or flower, a pet, a mountain or valley, or some other element of nature that leads to an aesthetic appreciation of our environs, the moment, and ultimately a larger, deeper reality. "One touch of nature," as Shakespeare reminds us, "makes the whole world kin."

So, go with the natural flow. You will find that reconnecting with Natural Time springs you from the trap of living in linear time, relieves stress, and brings a sense of space and clarity into your life. You will be one step closer to living in Buddha Standard Time.

In the next chapter we will delve more deeply into time's mysteries by reaching for our higher selves—our noblest, deepest natures—and learning more techniques for making peace with time.

CHAPTER 2

Taking Time for Your Higher Self

Leave the familiar for a while.
Let your senses and bodies stretch out . . .
Change rooms in your mind for a day.
All the hemispheres in existence
Lie beside an equator
In your heart.
Greet Yourself
In your thousand other forms
As you mount the hidden tide and travel
Back home.
All the hemispheres in heaven
Are sitting around a fire
Chatting
While stitching themselves together
Into the Great Circle inside of
You.

—Song of the Sufi mystic Hafiz

ONE DAY LAST YEAR I was driving a friend's daughter, Deena, to the airport. Deena was returning to college, and I asked her what she was studying and whether she had given much thought to what she would do after she graduated.

"I'm majoring in biology and ecological studies," she explained, "and I'd like to take a junior year abroad in one of the developing countries to find out how I might be able to help save an endangered species."

Wow, I thought. This young woman was already thinking more deeply about her life and what she could contribute than many seekers who have been trying to find themselves since the '60s and are still looking.

As you practice connecting with Natural Time and continue your journey toward living in Buddha Standard Time, you will learn, as Deena already has, to reach for your higher Self—in contrast to the small self, whose fleeting moods change from moment to moment. You don't have to be a Taoist sage, a high lama, a superhero, or the savior of an endangered species to lead a wise and fulfilling life. You just have to know how to monitor your energy and to constantly renew yourself in small ways throughout the day, as well as throughout the week and year.

We all play many roles in life: sibling, parent, child, spouse, neighbor, friend, citizen. But we are more than the sum of these parts. Our real self is none of these things. Our real self, our higher Self, transcends all evanescent roles, identities, and personas. And we can learn how to access it regularly.

It can be a challenge to find the time and space to live our higher Self. That nobler being within our deeper nature seeks, contemplates, and questions, whereas the era we live in is one of stops and starts and frequent interruptions. In some ways living our higher Self means coming to terms with how we experience ourselves in relation to time and the infinite. Perhaps the most important thing I learned from my sojourn in India and the Himalayas is that the divine dwells in each of us. It is deathless and beyond change or degeneration; it is timeless. Buddha lives in all of us and will guide us home to our true natures, if we are willing.

Gandhi's Watch

Buddhist wisdom tells us that *there is a level of consciousness or awakeful-ness within us that exists and operates independently of time,* transcending birth and death. In our day-to-day lives, though, we can feel we are noth-ing but a transient, ephemeral, conditioned conglomeration of our experi-ences and attitudes, dreams and hopes, fears and illusions. Yet it is indeed possible to embrace our higher natures, even as we remain bound by the time and space in which we live.

One of the things I discovered while living in ashrams, living a life based on Gandhi's teachings, is that Gandhi was devoted to his pocket watch—an eight-shilling Ingersoll timepiece that he attached to his waist with a safety pin and a string. Gandhi hated to be late and would often prop up the watch in front of him so that he could keep an eye on the time.

People often remarked that Gandhi seemed to always remain deeply absorbed, moment by moment, in whatever business he had at hand, no matter how significant or menial. Whether negotiating with the British viceroy or weaving his own clothes, he was focused on the task, remaining fully committed and engaged. Gandhi found that place of utter stillness, a place so potent he became the lever that dislodged the British Empire's imperial hold on his beloved India. This effective and charismatic leader liked to say that he was never tired because internally he was always at rest.

Gandhi and his philosophy of nonviolence exemplify the core value of what Buddhists call Right Livelihood—making a life, not just a living. (Right Livelihood is one of the tenets of the Buddhist Eightfold Path to Enlightenment; the other seven appear in chapter 5.) Gandhi walked his talk as a social activist and family man in this time- and space-bound world, even while his heart and mind were set upon the absolute world and universal deliverance.

The story about Gandhi's relationship with time is made more dra-matic by the fact that when he was assassinated, he fell on his watch and it broke, registering the exact minute of his death: 5:17 P.M. With the sound of gunshots still echoing around him, he blessed the man who had shot him. Gandhi died as he had lived, returning good for harm, practicing what he preached. His last words were his mantra: "Ram Ram," the name of God.

Gandhi is a perfect example of a person who has skillfully mastered both the small self's and the higher Self's experience of time. He managed a daily schedule effectively. He was clear about the purpose of his time on this earth and unafraid of death. And he devoted himself to healing the conflicted times in which he lived. His life and message were in perfect accord because he set his agenda and fulfilled it in each moment, living from his heartfelt convictions no matter what harm came his way. Gandhi directed all of his energy into finite, timely pursuits while at the same time drawing nourishment and inspiration from history and its sage prophets. With the power of living his commitments in every moment and accessing his higher Self, he changed the world.

Most of us are not going to be jailed for our beliefs or bring down empires, as Gandhi did. But with more sincere intention in the here and now, we can have an impact: give a smile, lend an ear, be more present- (rather than absent-) minded, reduce our carbon footprints, do what we can to genuinely loosen the hold of selfish greed, hatred, and illusion over our minds and hearts. And we can help ourselves by emulating Gandhi— seeking to recognize and balance the small self and the nobler highest inner Self within us. We can tend to temporal demands and be punctual, and still maintain contact with the eternal present in each moment.

A practical way to bring yourself closer to always "remembering to remember," or *re-mindfulness*, as I call it, is to repeat a mantra or, like Gandhi, the single syllable of God's name every day, sometimes aloud, sometimes within yourself, and move yourself closer to that high ground that both transcends and lies within each of us. Remembering to be mindful of your own breath—the most basic meditational tool—will give you another way to accomplish this from moment to moment. These simple methods will ground you to live more fully in the present and connect to a feeling of time-lessness rather than not having enough time. This life of mindful prayer will keep you centered and stable, and will allow you to live from the heart rather than just the head, connecting more fully with others.

Stuck in traffic and late for an appointment? Been on hold waiting to speak to someone for too long? There is nothing you can do about these modern-day annoyances, so there's no reason for your energy to turn neg-ative. There is a simple practice I do every day whenever I can, which I call WOW: Wishing Others Well. Whomever and whatever I meet—person or animal, male or female, old or young, human or otherwise—I wish them well. Make this your mission and delight from moment to moment.

Greet the world, as Gandhi did, with open hands, open arms, open heart, and open mind. This will make every single encounter meaningful, elevated, and truly connected to your deepest, highest, truest noble Self and soul.

Try sending heartfelt wishes and blessings at every single encounter, saying to yourself or even aloud:

May you be happy and peaceful, safe and blissful, content
and fulfilled, and always keep growing and glowing.
May you have all that you need and long for.
May your noble dreams come true for you.
May love flourish and blossom in your life.

How could we harm anyone while thinking or saying this? How could we manipulate or exclude or exploit anyone? Practicing WOW, you will release your feelings of aggravation with people who waste your time or irritate you. Wish Others Well, and feel your anger melt into kindness.

You'll find that it dramatically eases your own life, and you'll be surprised at how it improves your interactions with others.

Your Selves

The twenty-five-hundred-year-old Buddhist concept of *anatta* (literally, "no self") is just about the hardest nut to crack in Eastern philosophy, especially in an individualistic Western culture like ours that glorifies our imagined uniqueness. Yet everything about our individuality—our bodies, our thoughts and feelings, our predilections and intentions—is almost entirely conditioned, programmed by what went before, as well as subject to constant revision, transformation, improvement, and degradation over the course of our lives. We are a process, a work in progress. We are constantly *selfing* or cocreating each other and ourselves as we think we need to be in an effort to confirm our own existence and find security in a world that is inherently insecure and impermanent.

Anatta can also be translated as "no owner," as in: my thoughts (or my identity or my body) are not entirely mine; I did not produce them, nor do I govern them. We are, rather, a constellation of energies and forces held together by our egos and our will to survive, fed by an illusion of separateness. Beginning to understand this can free us from self-centeredness and open us to more evolved and compassionate ways of perceiving. Our smaller selves develop through genetics, socialization, family dynamics, peer pressure, and our own personal history—the last of which we are quite complicit in producing and maintaining along the way, through the constant process of selfing.

On the other hand, our true innate spiritual nature, or Buddha-nature, is beyond time and change. And the more we can embrace our uncorruptable Buddha-nature, the more we can appreciate our role in the huge and mysterious machine of time and space. Think of yourself as a cell in the great body of all human beings, and by extension of all beings everywhere, with whom you are inextricably connected.

When we don't recognize this inherent connection, it is easy to feel overwhelmed, unable to get each day's tasks done in the space of just one day. With one to-do list or another constantly bearing down on us, we try to achieve what can be finished in a short space of time. But in our long and wonderful lives, what we look back on with satisfaction is never the little pile of accomplishments—the report written, the laundry done, the lawn mowed—but the grander achievements, those of our higher Self, like the close connections we make with the important people in our lives, the children we raise, the slow mastery of a profession or craft, our contribution to a worthy cause.

It's hard to see this Big Picture as our days rush by in a blur. To make matters worse, many people have the added stress of being perfectionists. They can't just check something off their list and get it done. They feel compelled to double-check and even triple-check, which makes everything take longer than necessary when there doesn't seem to be enough time to begin with.

There's a very different kind of perfectionism, though, that is a trait worth striving for. *Dzogchen* (from *dzog,* meaning "perfect," and *chen,* meaning "great") is the highest teaching in the Tibetan tradition. *Dzogchen* is sometimes translated as the "Great Perfection," and it refers to the completeness of things just as they are—unity in diversity, and continuity amid change. To aspire toward glimpsing this Great Perfection, we need to stop projecting what appears in our own minds onto the outside world and instead allow ourselves to settle and just *be.*

That means detaching yourself from your thoughts, your anxieties, your dwelling upon the past and the future. Instead, experience your mind in its natural, unaltered state. This is exactly what we aim to do when we meditate. If you can manage this even when you're not in formal medi-tation, the barrier between yourself and others will evaporate, revealing empathy, love, compassion, and understanding. In this free and open state, you will be able to fill your life with the positive actions that will deliver happiness to you. Neither perfectionist nor ascetic, you will ease into the Middle Way.

This requires that you check in with yourself to see where your atten-tion is. Are you in a stupor, mindlessly watching TV or tied to your com-puter? Break yourself out of the trance by doing one physical task with focused attention, wholly and completely, while letting go of absolutely everything else. Unload the dishwasher or pile up the newspapers to recy-cle, but do it with every ounce of your attention. I find that doing this with full focus re-energizes me. As Zen master Thich Nhat Hanh put it so beau-tifully, "Washing the dishes is like bathing a baby Buddha. The profane is the sacred. Everyday mind is Buddha Mind."

Such "Full Connection Meditation," as I call it, collects all our scat-tered energies and dissipated thoughts and channels them into the produc-tion of one chore. The result is that we feel restored and fulfilled. When we practice and internalize the principle of Full Connection Meditation, we get the most out of every moment, whether at work or home, raking leaves, playing with a pet, conversing with a friend, making love, or making dinner. We can reap the rewards of this deep yet simple contemplation in action anywhere, anytime, with anyone. The better you get at it, the more you will understand one of the secrets to living in Buddha Standard Time: *It's not time that we lack, but focus.*

My friend Lynn, a life coach, has another simple but effective way to get back in touch with her higher Self. She tells me that when she feels overwhelmed, she gets up from her desk, places both hands on the back of the chair or on her belly or across her chest and heart area, and takes several deep breaths. She looks over her work area to get perspective before even considering returning to work. She stands for a little while, letting things settle and resolve themselves, letting some air and space into her awareness by just being, allowing the particles in the snow globe to settle and the scene within that great sphere to come into focus. After a few calm moments, she has a better sense of what she needs to do, and her day proceeds more harmoniously and effectively.

Close the door to your office and try this if you can. Rather than frittering away energy and wasting time, you will be helping make the rest of your day more productive and sharpening your problem-solving skills by calling on your higher Self.

The Wise Fisherman

The relation between the small self and higher Self is beautifully described in the Gnostic Gospel of Thomas. One of my favorite passages is verse 8, in which Jesus said, "The Man is like a wise fisherman who cast his net into the sea. He drew it up from the deep full of small fishes. Among them he found a big, marvelous fish. That wise fisherman, he threw all the smaller fishes back into the sea. He chose the big fish without hesitation. Whoever has ears to hear, let him hear."

The little fish are our momentary desires, ambitions, and goals: fortune, fame, pleasure, comfort, and other fleeting experiences. None of these can last. Yet we cling to them as if they will endure forever. The big fish is finding our eternal dream. Too many people fail to find the overarching purpose for their lives. They spend their days buffeted by their momentary desires and the chaotic forces around them. They are at the mercy of linear, sequential time, especially as it is measured today by clicks, texts, and tweets.

Those who find their passion in life—whether a profession or calling like teaching, a cause like the environment or human rights, a pastime like golf, or a role like being a good parent, neighbor, or friend—are so fully engaging their higher Selves that the hours and days pass quickly. They feel constantly fulfilled and renewed.

But even most passions have a limited life span. I think this is what Jesus is also hinting at. Dreams can die out, too, even such admirable and vital ones as parenting. What happens when the kids grow up and move away? Or when it's time for you to retire from your dream job? So what is the big fish—the biggest passion of all, the one that never ends? In the passage from Thomas, Jesus suggests that the biggest dream is the quest for and knowledge of God (or Allah or Buddha or Spirit or Moby Dick or whatever you like to call it). The foolish fishermen chase ephemeral things that result only in loss and suffering if they become dependent or cling to them. But the wise fisherman—like Deena, the college student—will throw back all the others and keep that one pure, radiant fish from the divine stream that gives life meaning and supreme joy.

Unfortunately, the disciples in these wisdom tales can't grasp Jesus's teaching about small self and higher Self (referred to throughout this Gospel as "me" and "Me," respectively). His listeners constantly mistake him for the predestined holy messiah, who will miraculously deliver them from Roman oppression and other forms of suffering. When his disciples asked: "When will the Kingdom come?" Jesus said: "It will not come by expectation. . . . But the Kingdom of the Father is spread over the earth and men see it not."

This is a perfect illustration of the difference between linear time and Buddha Standard Time. Deliverance, salvation, or enlightenment does not arrive in historical time. It is ever-present right here and now, in each and every moment. If we wait for it to come, it will never arrive. Jesus's approach to time and heaven is very similar to the Buddha's.

If the self is a constant act of creation, as Buddha and Jesus (as well as modern psychology) suggest, then on the grandest scale, beyond what you can ever imagine, your Self is a timeless, dynamic, creative force, abundantly powerful and divine. *As you let go of the small self in favor of your higher Self, your relationship to time will change.* In fact, we might say that the small self lives in ordinary sequential time, and the higher Self lives in Buddha Standard Time. Recognizing this within your own experience means appreciating each moment as part of a Greater Whole and letting go of notions about your limitations. You don't need to strive for the higher Self; it is already intrinsically yours. You just need to learn to open up to your Buddha-like, Christ-like, Allah-like being. And the small self, although never separate from the glorious whole, is what navigates the everyday world so that the higher Self can move beyond it.

We can use as many ways as we can find to reach our higher Self when the small one threatens to overwhelm us. Psychologist Mary Pipher, the author of *Reviving Ophelia,* among other best sellers, has said that she uses the sight and sound of birds as temple bells, reminders to take three deep breaths and reconnect with her Buddha-nature and with all living things. This practice helps her to slow down, relax, and create a transcendent moment. You can experiment with finding your own gateway to your higher Self. So many of us feel we are hurtling through the day, rarely free of the burden of stress over too many things to do and too little time. Take every opportunity you can to step off the treadmill and take a breather.

MINDFUL MOMENTS

Reaching for Your Higher Self

1. Run an *environmental scan* over your to-do list. I find this an important practice when I feel off center. In our Western culture that often measures quality and success by how many things we did in a day, how many places we visited, and how busy we were, I find it

restorative to take a step back and reflect. Consider all the things on your list that "must" be done, and ask yourself, "Really?"

2. When you're having trouble finding time to do what needs to be done, just take the next step. It's like driving in heavy snow: put the car in low gear, and just move forward—slow, grounded, and steady. Often, when you're overwhelmed or stuck, just taking one step is enough. You will always have time for just that one step. And then the next.

3. When you're overwhelmed by lack of time and too much to do, your mind can shut down, and it feels as if it's just you trying to accomplish all these things by yourself. But remember that we're all in this together and that we are always helping each other along the way. Notice that it's when you feel the whole burden on your shoulders alone that you have the strongest sense of urgency and panic. Try instead to recognize our interconnectedness. You are always part of a team, whether it's your coworkers, your family, your friends, or the universe of beings around you. They have all felt what you feel. Try saying softly to yourself, "We are all in this together."

4. Our breakneck pace can make us feel that *everything* is of the utmost urgency. Guess what? It's not. Realize that not every e-mail needs to be answered, or even opened, right away. Take a breath, and set the proper priorities that will enable you to get things done calmly. Assess the demands on you, and consider which ones are most important. Learn to say to yourself, "That can wait."

And don't forget to simply lighten up! I love the following story because it demonstrates that even the wisest spiritual teachers know the value of not taking themselves too seriously. One autumn, near Halloween, the

Dalai Lama was invited to speak at Yale University. That evening, the formal hosts, mostly august pedagogues in their somber academic robes and Phi Beta Kappa keys, came to get him for an important reception. After knocking on the door at his guesthouse, they were surprised to be greeted by a man in maroon and gold lama robes wearing a Groucho Marx mask, complete with eyeglasses, nose, and moustache. It was His Holiness the Dalai Lama himself, having a bit of All Hallows' Eve fun.

Finding Time in Losing Addictions

Among all the substances we misuse and abuse, the greatest is time. Our small self will do anything to save a few seconds or minutes, even if it squanders days and years of our lives. For example, rather than walk or bicycle to the café a half mile from home, my neighbor Fred prefers to drive his car. When you add up all the direct and indirect costs, including gas, mileage, wear and tear, insurance, taxes for road construction and maintenance, and carbon emissions and other climate control, it costs Fred far more than the few dollars he spends on his newspaper and cappuccino.

Walking, of course, could be much more beneficial. It strengthens our lungs, intestines, and all other organs, systems, and functions of the body. It acclimates us to the elements, allowing us to better adjust to extremes of hot and cold (and thereby lower our thermostats at home and save even more time and money). Walking heightens our senses, stimulates our awareness, relaxes our mind, enlivens our energy, and puts us in touch with nature. Even on familiar walks, there is always something new and fresh, or an old and adored friend or acquaintance—human, animal, or meteorological—that crosses our path. Rather than a distraction or waste of time, walking is a natural meditation, a break during the day to treasure, and an investment in a healthful, long-lived future. Walking to the store every day instead of driving might even help prevent a heart attack.

When you think about it, our conventional addictions—to coffee, soda, cigarettes, chocolate, sugar, alcohol, drugs, and the like—for the most part arise in an effort to balance or control time. We take caffeine in the morning, and often throughout the day, to wake up, stay alert, stimulate our creativity, juggle our schedule, keep from falling asleep, and otherwise stay productive when we might not feel productive. We smoke cigarettes to calm down, relax, and improve our focus, especially if we have a stressful occupation or a boring, repetitive job in which time slows to a crawl and we need breaks to relieve the tedium. We devour chocolate and other sugary snacks to both stimulate us and numb the pain and frustration of the daily grind or an emotional upset. Our blood-sugar levels soar, life's impermanency is temporarily forgotten, and the things we can't change no longer matter—at least for the few minutes that the euphoria lasts. We drink and take drugs to drown our sorrows from attachments to things that time has taken from us or that we have let pass by, and to ease our worries about the future. These substances allow us to escape into a chemically induced fantasy world where time appears to stop and everything is pleasurable and comforting.

Of course, the benefits of our addictions are short-lived and require ever larger doses to have the same effect. As a result, our health suffers, our consciousness clouds over, and we become more and more dependent on substances that distort our orientation to time and space. The Buddhist way to overcome stress and unease is to use *skillful means*—effectively and appropriately engaging in what needs to be done.

I know a young professional woman with a stressful job. "At the end of the day," Marian told me, "I just want to crash in front of the TV with a bottle of wine." That's how she spent most evenings, and then she would go to sleep and begin the cycle all over again. Other people zone out on the Internet. These are clearly not ways that will replenish us for the day ahead. Instead, I urged

Marian to try taking a brisk walk, eating natural, home-cooked foods, meditating, engaging in vigorous exercise or the martial arts, making or listening to music, painting, taking photos, writing a poem or blog, or experimenting with other ways that put her in touch with her higher Self. If Marian pursues these activities in Full Connection Meditation, she will feel fully refreshed and replenished, and able to apply skillful means to her life's work.

Perhaps the biggest crutch of the current age is our electronics addiction—our inability to wean ourselves from the constant stimulation of technological information and entertainment. Every e-mail we receive, every iTune we download, every text conversation we have with a friend triggers feelings of enjoyment by unleashing a spurt of dopamine in our brain's pleasure center. This neurotransmitter, also released by food and sex, is responsible for feelings of reward and satisfaction, and we are hardwired to love such experiences. But just as our need for salt and sugar led to unprecedented health and weight problems when foods overloaded with these ingredients became cheaply available, our delight in connecting and interacting with our computers, smartphones, iPods, and other devices has reached a point where it's often stealing time instead of giving us more.

A recent *Newsweek* article quoted clinical psychologist Adam J. Cox explaining that half a century ago one might have become bored after a couple of hours with no activity. Today a young person can feel bored after *thirty seconds* with nothing to do. Children are growing up with near-constant interaction with one electronic device or another. That leaves no time for wondering, exploring, socializing, analyzing, or self-reflection. What this is doing to their sense of time can only be guessed, but it seems to me that future generations may lose out on the treasures of the higher Self such as having nuanced relationships with other people, focusing on a book that might change their life, and otherwise seeking the examined life that is our birthright.

As adults, we are constantly consuming information. Some people even take their BlackBerry into the bathroom with them. As we go from screen to screen in our homes, in our cars, at the office, and in all of the places in between, we are cutting time up into thinner and thinner slices until it slips right through our fingers. We are losing the concept of taking a break, whether we're on vacation but still check e-mail five times a day or we never take an interval between activities to slow down and just be. And scientists say that without real downtime, we are not able to solidify our experiences into full-fledged memories. The nonstop digital influx is making us tired and using up every spare moment. We do ourselves a disservice by killing time in this way.

We deserve better. How can we resist what seems an irresistible way of life today—the adrenaline rush that accompanies each beep? Once again, by giving full attention to each thing we encounter. Full Connection Meditation—as many times a day as you can do it—is the antidote to the techno-addiction that fragments our focus. Step away from your computer, put down your handheld device, and concentrate on the green earth around you, the laugh of a child floating in through the window, your own life-breath.

One of the most exciting recent discoveries in the neurochemistry of the brain is that meditation increases the production of serotonin, a neurotransmitter that positively influences mood, behavior, and emotional well-being. The implication of these studies is that meditation offers a safe, natural way to unwind, calm down, and stabilize one's mood. Aside from daily stress and anxiety, low serotonin levels are associated with a wide range of disorders, including obesity, insomnia, narcolepsy, sleep apnea, migraine headaches, premenstrual syndrome, and fibromyalgia. If larger numbers of people meditated, there could be a significant reduction in the use of Prozac and other antidepressants, whose use has skyrocketed in recent years. If you are taking an antidepressant or antianxiety drug, consider incorporating meditation into your life on a regular basis. By connecting regularly with your higher Self in this way, you might find, in consultation with your physician, that you need a lower dosage of the drug, or none at all.

Part of a Larger Whole

In *The Biology of Belief,* cellular biologist Bruce Lipton writes about the scientific basis for the mind–body connection and points out this marvel: a single human cell is like a microcosm of the entire human being. By extension, I'd say that each human being is a microcosm of the entire species.

Now imagine identifying each of us as cells being played out in the body of the Greater Whole—the universe beyond space and time. We are inextricably connected with other communities or systems: our family system, our friends and colleagues, our culture, our country, and the entire planet, solar system, and galactic universe. There is only a small genetic difference between humans and apes. And only a small difference between the chemical structure of hemoglobin in red blood and that of chlorophyll in a plant. Isn't this interconnectedness of beings astonishing?

It's not easy, in our empirical, materialistic, and rational information-based culture, to intuitively feel this intrinsic relationship with the entire chain of being. But when we can come to experience the power of that connection, we find that it erases boundaries, small-mindedness, and fearful, cloudy thinking and emotions. The web and diversity of life remind me of Albert Schweitzer's philosophy of reverence for life. In the middle of Africa, the great physician discovered his commonality with all that is. "I am life that wills to live in the midst of life that wills to live," he observed. For fifty years, he labored tirelessly in the hot equatorial sun, treating patients suffering from leprosy, dysentery, and other infectious conditions who flocked to his free jungle clinic. The good doctor also kept a lively menagerie at his hospital and befriended many creatures, among them a pet pelican. Visitors, in anecdotes reminiscent of stories about the Buddha and Saint Francis, invariably remarked about how birds, animals, and even insects flocked to his kindly presence.

Schweitzer is another great example of someone who could distinguish between the self and the Self. As a young man, he had become celebrated throughout Europe as a theologian and an organist. His book on the historical Jesus challenged Protestantism, and his concerts of Bach's music were unequalled. Yet living the life of a theological giant and musical celebrity was not who he was. Looking within, he realized that his deepest Self would be manifested in a life of compassion and serving others. In the spirit of the Wise Fisherman, he threw fame and fortune back into the sea. To his amazement, Schweitzer became even more renowned when he forsook modern civilization for the African jungle, but being the world's most famous doctor never went to his head. Eventually he won the Nobel Peace Prize for the ethical and moral example that he set. During the Cold War, scientists claimed that nuclear fallout was no more dangerous than the luminous dial of a wristwatch, provoking Schweitzer to speak out eloquently. "Truth has no special time of its own," he declared, summing up his own fully engaged approach to life. "Its hour is now—always."

As time-bound beings, we need to go through the progressive stages of growth, from childish dependence to adult independence, before we can realize our intrinsic interdependence and the autonomy and freedom of our higher Self. This is simply healthy psychological development. Carl Jung said that the first half of our lives is spent developing an egoic self, and proposed that the second half be devoted to transcending it. A child is not ready to transcend the ordinary, everyday self because he or she is still developing one. But we shouldn't disparage the small self. It is, after all, a part of our higher Self in the same way that time is part of the timeless. Think of your small self as a gleam in the eye of your Buddha-nature.

Onward and inward, I like to say. Growing up, and growing "in," to become your authentic self can be a real challenge. First, you have to strive to recognize and acknowledge the limitations of your small self and compassionately *accept* all your warts, because denying or ignoring your problems sidesteps the issue at great cost. In this moment, could you easily list your likes and dislikes, inclinations, aversions, bad habits and good sense, hot buttons, blind spots and prejudices, greatest hits and flops? Try it. For the basic principle of enlightened living is seeing things as they are.

While retaining a modicum of healthy self-esteem—that is the Middle Way—you should not allow yourself to feel that you are more special than anyone or anything else. And thinking you're worse than others is simply another form of narcissism. For rest assured, none of us, neither saint nor sinner, is closer to God or Buddha than any other; we all possess Buddha-nature. How can we be any closer to our higher Selves, which are already closer to us than our breath and our blood?

TIME OUT

A Drop into Stillness

This is a thought experiment in seeking our true nature and the relationship between self and Self, time and timelessness. It will help you experience a deeper reality amid the impermanence of life and let go of the stress, hindrances, and distractions that cloud your self-identity and awareness.

Begin with the reading, and then pause and listen to the silence afterward.

Take a few deep breaths and drop into stillness.

Breathe, Smile, Relax

Let go.

Let be.

Now ask:

My body—what endures?

That which I think and feel and understand—what endures?

That which I like and dislike—what endures?

That which I will and intend—what endures?

In my capacity to hear, see, smell, taste,

and in my physical and mental capacity—what endures?

And when I

Let the body go;

Let my thoughts and feelings go;

Let likes and dislikes go;

Let will-force and intentions go;

Let hearing, seeing, smelling, tasting, physical and mental capacity go—

What remains?

Who am I, beyond my body and analytical mind,

personality, self-image, and history?

Who continues as I go through all the stages and passages of life,

from childhood to youth, teens, young adulthood,

middle years, old age, and on into the future?

What, if anything, can I find

to ground Myself

in my true Self,

my most irreducible essence?

Ask the Question:

Who and what am I, really, beneath it all?

Who or what might continue on when my body turns to dust?

Who or what am I right now?

What time is it really?

Let the silence resound with this question.

Make Time for Your Life

I hope the previous experiment in contemplating the impermanence of your small self helped you realize the importance of connecting to your higher Self. Otherwise, life can just unroll like a crazy quilt before us and we miss the best part of the ride, the soaring, magic-carpet flight to realms of self-discovery, self-realization, and connection to all beings.

We must remind ourselves to remember our higher Self amid the rush and busyness of life. Here is a Buddhist verse that I like to repeat when I feel stressed and overwhelmed by chores and demands:

I choose not to waste time on empty desires.
I vow to overcome craving for experience.
And when I do I feel an upsurge in energy, spacious attention,
and clarity,
Thus arises the understanding and time to do what has to be done.

When we choose to step away from our culture's addiction to increasingly grandiose forms of consumption and competition, we find all kinds of satisfaction and contentment through freedom and autonomy, including extra energy, extra time, and extra space in a new and different quality of life. Who doesn't have time for such rich forms of experience?

My friend Janet, the head of a Christian foundation, a Sunday school teacher and mother, told me that her productivity and ever ready, willing, and able busyness—although at times an asset—can become an obstacle. When she feels overwhelmed, Janet remembers just to stop, pause, breathe once or twice, and then ask herself, "What is the most important thing to be done in this moment?"

When she first started trying to meditate, she would find that by the end of the day she hadn't done it. It wasn't that she didn't have the time; rather, it was because she didn't make it a priority. Yet even with all her work and being a parent to boot, she eventually found that there were always twenty minutes in the day to just sit and reconnect to her Self—if she made sure it happened. And she found that doing nothing but meditating for twenty minutes made all the other minutes of the day go more smoothly, with greater ease and clarity.

"Instead of going on autopilot as soon as the alarm went off," she recounts, "I slowly started to check in with myself throughout the day and began noticing where my attention was being focused. As I became more aware, it struck me how much of my attention was not actually on the present moment. When I became more mindful of the here and now, it helped ground me, and transformed the entire direction of my life. When my daughter was having an emotional crisis in college, I felt raw and terrified. How could I best support her in each moment? How could I best support myself? Mindfulness, prayer, and meditation practice is what got me through it."

Physiologically, meditation techniques that enhance mindfulness have an incredibly calming effect, increasing activity in the prefrontal cortex and reducing activity in the amygdala—the organs that play a role in the processing and memory of emotional reactions. Janet's regular practice allowed her to choose and act wisely even in moments of high stress.

Here is a practice, called Simply Being, to help put you in touch with your deeper, more authentic Self. It will help you see that you are perfect right now, just as you are: no more striving, no more struggle, no more inner tensions or conflicts.

Simply Being

Sit comfortably.
Perhaps close your eyes or lower your gaze.
Take a deep breath or two and relax.
Breathe slowly and let it all go.
Release the tension and relax a little more.
Stop doing and settle
back into just being. Let
things settle without your
direction or intercession.
Let go. Wherever things
fall is OK for now. Open
to the wisdom of allowing,
of inclusive acceptance.
Befriend yourself; familiarize yourself with your own
fundamental presence. Let awareness be uninterrupted
by techniques or concepts.
If and when you feel lost, distracted, spaced out, or
sleepy, get in touch with your breath. Watch the breath;
observe the inhalation and exhalation as they effortlessly
occur. Feel the breath moving in and out, anchoring you in
the present moment while you again let everything go,
without judgment, evaluation, or interference.
Opening gradually to the effortlessness of pure
presence; turn your attention inward. All we seek can
be found within. This is the process and practice of
inner freedom.
Being Buddha, being yourself,
Being all.

Research into meditative exercises like this one has recently found startling insights into the nature of the self, especially in its relation to time and space. In studies of the frontal lobes of Tibetan meditators, Andrew Newberg, M.D., reports that he has been able to isolate the areas that are most active by measuring blood flow with an advanced brain-imaging technology called SPECT (single photon emission computed tomography). Dr. Newberg's tests demonstrate that the front part of the brain, which is usually involved in focusing attention and concentration, is much more active during meditation. He also found decreased activity in the parietal lobe, the area of the brain that gives us a sense of being oriented in space and time.

Dr. Newberg found that when the meditator focuses inward and this area of the brain is deprived of sensory input, the sense of self ends—there is no longer a "border between the self and the world." Far from being a psychological or spiritual state, the researchers found that the perception of the self as "one with all of creation" had a neurological foundation and was experienced as "utterly real."

What a wonderful convergence of modern science and spirituality! Neuroscience has quantified the disappearance of a boundary between self and cosmos in the meditating brain.

High Man on the Totem Pole

Where are you? In the fragments of memories, diaries, correspondence, pictures, movies, and videos of yourself at different stages of your life? Or in the mirror, where everything is two-dimensional and reversed? The real you will never, ever be captured. If you're like most people, seeing a photograph of yourself or hearing your voice on tape makes you uncomfortable. "That's not what I look [or sound] like!" you say. Everything we do and create is like an entry in our diary or Facebook page: that moment's manifestation of self. You can look at thirty images of yourself from a photo session and find maybe one that comes close to capturing you. We are all of ourselves and none of ourselves. As the poet said, "I contain multitudes."

The native peoples of the Pacific Northwest dealt with this artistic and spiritual challenge through the totem pole. Although there are many kinds of totem poles, including ones that depict ancestors, kinfolk, heroes, and mythological creatures, the carvings typically depict the stages of self-development. The hierarchical unfolding of this process has entered our vocabulary with the expression "low man on the totem pole." Spiritually, this signifies our small or everyday self, while the carving at the top symbolizes our highest, most evolved sacred Self. Just beneath the topmost face, there is usually a large pair of wings extending horizontally. These symbolize the soul taking flight into the realm beyond time and space. Together, the totem's many faces—arranged like the chakras, or natural energy centers in the body—point to the whole or totality of being and the rising, upward process of awakening, growth, and maturity, reaching our full, majestic potential.

To see the whole, you need the panoramic view from atop the totem pole. That requires overcoming the distractions in your day that keep you from seeing and embracing your higher Self. And *that* requires finding eternity in the crystalline present moment, being 100 percent engaged in your current activity. To live in Buddha Standard Time, you'll need to find moments throughout the day when you can transcend your smaller self. Thus in the smallest action you will be reaching as high and as deep as you can.

In chapter 3, you will learn to synchronize linear time and cyclical time, attune to the chakras and natural circadian rhythms of your body, and listen to your innermost heartbeat—the most reliable timepiece you have.

CHAPTER 3

Getting in Sync

To see a world in a grain of sand,
And a heaven in a wild flower,
Hold infinity in the palm of your hand,
And eternity in an hour.

—William Blake

ONE OF THE BEST perspectives on the mysteries of time comes from Jill Bolte Taylor, a Harvard-trained neuroscientist who suffered a massive stroke at the age of thirty-seven. In her fascinating book, *A Stroke of Insight: A Brain Scientist's Personal Journey*, she narrates her harrowing experience and the eight years it took her to rebuild her life. As doctors discovered, Taylor had a clot the size of a golf ball that completely shut down the left hemisphere of her brain.

In the space of just four hours, Taylor observed her own mind completely deteriorate to the point where she could not walk, talk, read, write, or recall. As the damaged left side of her brain—our rational, grounded, detail- and time-oriented side—lost much of its function, she alternated between two realities: the associative, creative right brain, which retained a sense of complete well-being and peace during the whole ordeal; and the analytical left brain, which observed her undergoing the stroke and was nimble enough to seek help in time.

After her recovery, in searching for words to explain what it's like to remember living completely in her right brain, Taylor reverted to child-like wonder: "It's kind of like the story of how the blue sky is always there, and so I see the blue sky as the right hemisphere. It's always there. It's always doing what it does. It's a constant entity. The left hemisphere is the clouds and the clouds represent brain chatter. The clouds come in, and the thoughts come in, and they block the view of being able to see the blue sky even though the blue sky is always there." It's interesting that her description of the left and right brain hemispheres correlates to the relationship we've examined between the little self and higher Self.

During the initial stages of her recovery, Taylor felt lost in the blue sky, and to be functional in her daily life she had to consciously choose to bring the clouds back. Like some people with near-death experiences who return from a world of radiance and light, she had to consciously will herself back into the ordinary world. In the course of healing, as the logical left brain started to mend, she learned to switch back and forth from one hemisphere to the other. Through visualization, she began to strengthen or rewire her own neural circuitry. It required tremendous will and effort, because floating in the boundless blue sky felt so satisfying and peaceful.

Taylor ultimately perceived her eight-year period of illness and recovery as a gift rather than a waste of time. It made her realize that the key to living a fulfilling life is recognizing the need to synchronize both sides of the brain, and she writes that her life is far more gratifying as a result. We need the left brain to analyze, evaluate, make decisions, strategize, and execute. But we also need the right brain to dream, imagine, see patterns, express our feelings, and rejoice. No one can be exclusively right- or left-brained (at least not for long). "It's time to bust out of the box and decide we have a whole brain and it's a beautiful thing," she declared.

A chief difference between the two halves has to do with experiencing and managing time. In the left-brain mode, Taylor experienced almost constant stress and pressure. In the right-brain mode, there was no measurement of time (an insight that complements the research by Andrew Newberg that I mentioned in the last chapter). She felt free to create, dream, and enjoy without any urgency.

Fortunately, there is a natural bridge between the two halves of the brain that prevents us from living exclusively in one hemisphere or the other. It's a tiny cable of nerves called the corpus callosum. We might say it unifies our head and our heart, our mind and our emotions, our masculine and feminine energies.

In describing her extraordinary experience, over and over again Taylor uses terms like "timelessness," "interconnectedness," "in the moment," "the big picture," "blissful," and "peace"—words that are found primarily in psychic and mystical literature. As this once high-achieving, type-A, Harvard-educated intellectual discovered, there was no scientific lexicon to draw from in describing her experience. She had to resort to basic vocabulary. Later her inquiry to make sense of it all took her to traditional spiritual and metaphysical teachings, especially Buddhism.

Taylor's work concludes with a summary of current medical studies with Tibetan meditators and Franciscan nuns. Interestingly, like the dots in the yin and yang symbol, the latest neurological research shows that cheerfulness, enthusiasm, and feeling full of energy are governed by the left prefrontal cortex, while anxiety, anger, and depression are localized in the right prefrontal cortex—the reverse of what we might expect. The studies show, however, that meditation strengthens the nerve fibers of the corpus callosum and deepens communication between the two hemispheres.

Taylor's way of explaining freedom from time pressures as a radiant, immaculate blue sky periodically clouded over by dark thoughts and anxieties is not especially Buddhist or religious, nor is it particularly scientific or even psychological. But millennia of Tibetan meditations and comparable contemplative ceremonies and practices among the Maya, the ancient Celts, the Hopi, and the shamans of other indigenous peoples support her experience, underlining the inherent unity of East and West, traditional wisdom and modern science, and the light and dark sides of our psyches.

Father Time and Mother Earth

In the first two chapters, we learned how to enter the realm of Natural Time and to connect to our higher Self. Now, we'll look at ways to get in sync with both linear and cyclical time—an important stage in the journey to balance, wholeness, and realizing our full potential. We'll explore the relationship between Father Time and Mother Earth within ourselves, and how the wisdom teachings of Buddhism can help us make peace with time by coming back into centeredness and equilibrium. We will look at how to balance left- and right-brain thinking and behavior as well as how to align the chakras, and we will discover the best times of day for realizing our optimal potential and well-being.

Just as Jill Bolte Taylor experienced a dramatic demonstration of the two hemispheres of the brain, we have historically thought of time and nature as dualities, even assigning them different sexes. In Western mythology, the figure of Father Time is an ancient, white-bearded man with a scythe and an hourglass through which the sands of time run. In the West, Father Time is often paired with Mother Nature or Mother Earth, the archetype of the Goddess that becomes manifest in all aspects of our lives as nurturing energy, one who looks after us, the ground of existence, and the womb of creativity. We all derive from and return to her.

The sacred feminine principle and vital female energy play a powerful role in the higher Buddhist teachings, which strive to balance masculine and feminine, solar and lunar polarities. She is the very image and embodiment of *Prajna Paramita,* the highest wisdom; *shunyata,* vast emptiness, infinite openness; and warm, all-embracing, compassionate spaciousness. In fact, in Buddhist literature supreme wisdom is called the Venerable Mother, the womb of enlightenment, because it is *the* great mystery, our primal essence.

Think of how much energy you have when you are nurturing or being nurtured. We must give to receive, and we must laugh, cry, think, and feel every day to be truly alive and well. It's not hard to recognize that love and gratitude are instrumental in replenishing us when we feel drained. How much of our cultural addiction to sex, television, the Internet, and other transient outlets for novelty and entertainment, for example, comes from loneliness and a lack of the powerful, active, attentive awareness-wisdom energy of the Divine Mother? As the Dalai Lama reminds us, "Everywhere we are constantly talking about peace for humanity. A peaceful world. But this is not from prayer, not from technology, not from money, not from religion, but from Mother." A harmonious planet and a tranquil soul come from the essence of mothering: compassion, nurturing, and love.

Father Time is linear time, the sands running out grain by grain in an endless stream. Buddhism calls this finite reality "relative time." It's the story or movie we play out as the years roll by: keeping our daily schedule, planning ahead, learning from the past, and making forward progress. Father Time represents the tirelessly dynamic and inventive quest for improvement, novelty, and achievement. This sacred masculine or yang energy embodies *doing.*

In contrast, Mother Nature represents cyclical earth time, the seasonal round, the phases of the moon, the rhythms of day and night, the passage from birth to death, and other beginnings and endings that repeat themselves endlessly. Mother Nature represents the wisdom and insight born of experience, of repetition, of practice, and of the tried and true. This sacred feminine energy embodies *being*. But as the Goddess, the formless and divine source of All, she is also Absolute Time, Great Time, the dimension of time that extends without beginning or end. And think about it: if there is no beginning or end, can we say that time exists? Where are its borders? What stands beside or outside of it? Time is like space—from which, science tells us, it's inseparable, both boundless and groundless.

Time is. And is not. A nice Zen question: how is this possible? The answer is "Both. And." And this is what wholeness feels like. This is our balancing act. A little insight from novelist Maxine Hong Kingston: "I learned to make my mind large, as the universe is large, so that there is room for contradictions."

Little Mind and Big Mind

Through meditation, we can find the still center of our true being, synchronizing Father Time and Mother Earth. Buddhist terms like *awareness*, *centeredness*, and *mindfulness* all point to evolved qualities of realization that have been developed beyond the purely instinctual level and the realm of reactivity, bringing us to a level of *conscious living*. We control and manage what we pay attention to if we learn how to take charge of our lives in an intelligent and appropriate manner: fully sensitive and attuned.

Being distracted, as we saw in the last chapter, is a major reason for feeling stressed and burned out by life roaring by. You cannot live completely in the moment when your mind is darting in all different directions. But when you can concentrate your attention and focus fully on what you are actually feeling and doing, in the immediacy of the present, moment by moment, the effects of whatever you do, intend, pray for, or aspire to will be powerful and lasting. There are practical techniques you can apply when you feel frazzled and need to find focus.

Try to do something that is the *opposite* of the task you've been working on. Remember that it's beneficial to give both sides of your brain a chance to work out. If you've been busy using your left brain for intense analytical thinking while studying or working, revitalize yourself by calling on the right brain. Listen to some music, for example, let your eyes rest on some beautiful art, or call a supportive friend for some emotional sustenance. If you're one of the many people who sit in front of a computer for most of the day, try doing some stretches or squats to clear the mind-path and restore energy. Just as experts tell us that the close computer work many of us do should be offset by staring into the distance every once in a while or getting up to walk around, it's important to alternately stimulate the hemispheres of your brain. This alternation helps counterbalance and reharmonize the two hemispheres and their yin and yang energies and puts you in sync with the natural flow of energy and time.

Don't discount the possibility that you are putting unnecessary pressure on yourself. Sometimes I'm working hard, say, to get something to the post office before it closes, only to realize that one more day won't make much difference. Ask yourself, Will it really change anything if this gets done a little later, or tomorrow? If not, relax and work out a realistic schedule. If so, keep going, but intersperse the task with brief exercise, meditation, breath, or phone breaks, and don't worry that they're keeping you from your work, because they're not: they're enabling you to complete it.

Try the following tips for making peace with time in other situations.

1. WHEN YOU WAKE UP, STOP YOURSELF FROM THINKING "WHAT DO I NEED TO DO TODAY?" and feeling the burden all at once. Just rest for a moment, awake and aware. Take a deep, invigorating breath. Then do the next thing to begin your day.

2. LISTEN TO YOUR INNER VOICE. If it's shouting, "You need to get this done!" try to notice that thought without feeling driven and utterly overwhelmed by it. Be sure to take pauses throughout the day without thinking of what you should be doing. There is an art to feeling comfortable while unmoored, to rest in the still eye of the storm.

3. EVERY TIME THE PHONE RINGS, LET IT GO FOR AN EXTRA RING OR TWO. Instead of rushing to pick it up, use it as a found moment to renew your nowness-awareness. Then get on with the call. Zen master Thich Nhat Hanh recommends that we use the extra telephone rings, or a moment after the doorbell rings, as a little mindfulness bell, to remind us to slow down, calm and clear our mind, and take a moment to breathe, smile, and relax.

TIME OUT

Breathing Fire

For relief and release from time stress, try the yogic Breath of Fire.
Take a deep breath,
entirely filling your lower belly . . .
and then release the breath with a huge whoosh of relief.
Rapidly repeat this breath of fire seven times,
or even twenty-one times, harmonizing your mind and body and
energy.
And then let your breath settle naturally,
allowing the gentle tide of breathing to wash in and out
through your being; relax entirely
and just be.

Mindfulness is the main ingredient in Buddha's practical, universally applicable recipe for a life of enlightened awakefulness. Mindfulness focuses the mind, then it eases the mind, and finally it realizes the lucid, spiritual nature and radiant clarity of mind itself. Shantideva, the Peace Master of ancient India, said: "If you tether to positive thoughts the wild elephant of the mind with the rope of mindfulness, all dangers will disappear and all virtues come into your hands."

There are three basic meditation practices for transforming our limited life experience, with its narrow frame of reference, to one that's in sync—blessed with wholeness, wisdom, clarity, peace, and joy.

The First Practice: Concentration

We are born with the capacity to be conscious of what is going on around and within us. But everything would appear chaotic, fuzzy, and undifferentiated if we didn't have an innate ability to discriminate one thing from another and discern subtle differences in order to make decisions, learn lessons, and connect the dots to pick up underlying patterns and principles. We can focus our minds to get the details—typical rational, linear, left-brain activity—and we can also intuit all at once entire situations and larger perspectives, characteristic of the right brain. With intentional practice, we can hone and sharpen our ability to discern multiple levels of awareness, and awaken the mind while opening the heart.

The practice of *concentrative meditation* serves just this purpose: as we train our awareness to focus on just one thing to the exclusion of all else, our capacity to pay attention overall becomes more and more refined, our attention span lengthens, and we more easily manage to push distractions to the side and stay fixed on the object of our interest. When we focus all our attention on one thing, the ripples of that acute concentration extend out to enhance our performance at everything.

The simple practice of concentrating on the breath helps hone, focus, and sustain the attention, in the same way that gathering the light of the sun with a magnifying glass can set a pile of leaves ablaze. Think of your concentration as the lens that magnifies and focuses the light of awareness into a laserlike beam. You might not manage to set leaves on fire, but you will be sharpening and refining your mental powers and abilities.

The Second Practice: Mindfulness

The second key to accessing the radiant state of nowness is to take responsibility for what you pay attention to and become more intentional, mindful, objective, and observant. Become interested in, but not attached to, the minutiae of your life, your transient experiences. Learn to observe it all in a state of vast, open-minded awareness, like Taylor's clouds passing through the clear, calm sky—appreciating things as they are, but with appropriate boundaries and a wide-angle perspective. Concentration brings your attention to a pinpoint focus, and mindfulness leads you deeper into the fabric and texture of temporal reality.

The practice of mindful meditation is how we increase our ability to learn self-control and mental discipline, transform our attitude, and shift toward being more responsive, thoughtful, intentional, and aware. Let me describe it this way: after forty years of daily meditation, I'm more like the warm and caring grandparent than the overinvested parent watching nervously as the children play.

The Third Practice: Insightfulness

As we increase our ability to concentrate and be more mindful, intuitive insights flood in. This is the third practice: accessing the truth of who we really are and how we fit in by refining our field of awareness. The benefits of this insight are increased through the practice of deep seeing and self-inquiry meditation. In insightfulness, one eases into the meditation, contemplates one's surroundings, and reflects on the mind that is meditating.

This practice is further deepened through enhancement practices such as what I call the art of *presencing,* an even more active and immediate level of nowness-awareness that we will look at in chapter 5.

Self-knowledge is power and a key to getting in sync. Thus Socrates exhorted his students and the people of Athens to know themselves. The more we know and learn about our selves, the less we are attached to and fearful of the idea that our days are numbered. As Oliver Wendell Holmes reminds us, "A mind that is stretched by a new experience can never go back to its old dimensions."

The Art of Synchrony

The word *synchrony* literally means "together in time." The practice of meditation is a beautiful way to bring our left-brain hemisphere (governed by Father Time) and our right-brain hemisphere (Mother Earth's bailiwick) into a perfect synchrony of Doing and Being. Concentrative meditation focuses on linear or left-brain thinking. Mindfulness meditation focuses the mind even more strongly, intensifying the natural electromagnetic charge to the rational, left hemisphere while integrating the intuitive, holistic right-brained activity. When performed regularly, mindfulness meditation will deliver extraordinary gifts of understanding and self-realization. Insightfulness meditation engages the associative right brain, and the intense concentration can result in a spontaneous release of restriction into sudden expansion. A burst of cyclical or spiraling insight arises, and proportionately more energy flows to the right hemisphere, bringing about breakthrough insights and intuitive discoveries. We are in sync— left with a synthesis of linear and cyclical thought, a balance of contraction and expansion, logic and intuition, which is the perfect harmony of yang and yin. We become illumined.

We might say for the sake of simplicity that the left brain is our head's mind and the right brain is our heart's mind. And each has its own logic. Let's say we want to study the workings of our solar system and universe. The left-brain approach is to make an outline of celestial objects, define each, and then analyze, quantify, and theorize about its formation. The right-brain approach is to glance over charts and maps of the heavens, make a poster, mobile, or diorama, or simply go outside at night and, as Walt Whitman said, look "up in perfect silence at the stars." Gradual progress comes from linear, regular, repetitive practice of any skill, including attention and awareness training. Insight more commonly comes all at once, replicating the gestalt or intuitive learning style of the right side of the brain. Both are needed.

Regular meditative practice increases our spiritual epiphanies and breakthrough peak experiences. With discipline and effort, a trigger will suddenly allow for simultaneous awareness and realization. We still the mind to one-pointed focus, and instead of narrowing down to the one point, it broadens out as far as it can. How extraordinary to go small and end up in infinity. This is the joy and wisdom that meditation can bring you. As J. Krishnamurti, the great spiritual educator, has observed: "Meditation is the ending of thought. It is only then that there is a different dimension that is beyond time."

Tuning Up Your Circadian Rhythms

Sundials, hourglasses, watches, alarm clocks, and other mechanical timepieces are in the grand scheme of things all relatively recent inventions, but human beings have biological clocks that date back to the earliest evolution of our species. Indeed, all sentient beings, including plants, animals, birds, reptiles, and bacteria, are governed by a roughly twenty-four-hour cycle known as a circadian rhythm.

Circadian rhythms regulate blood pressure, body temperature, wakefulness, sleep, and other metabolic processes. The master biological clock is located in the hypothalamus, a tiny endocrine gland in a group of cells known as the suprachiasmatic nucleus (SCN). There are also independent circadian rhythms located in many organs and cells, including the liver, lungs, pancreas, spleen, skin, and thymus. Like honeybees and migrating birds, monarch butterflies have an internal clock in their antennae that makes use of a sun compass, allowing them to correct their flight direction as the sun moves across the sky while they migrate from the East Coast and Midwest to wintering grounds in central Mexico every autumn. The built-in compass compensates for the change in light they experience traversing several time zones.

The master clock in the SCN generally follows cycles between 23.5 hours and 24.65 hours, or just about our ordinary day. Scientific studies of Tibetan monks and of Western volunteers living in dark caves for months show that our body's circadian rhythms are independent of light, darkness, temperature, food, water, and other external stimuli. This is related to the internal energies that mirror external phenomena such as sunrise and moonrise. Generally, however, the SCN is reset each day to the earth's twenty-four-hour cycle of rotation on its axis by exposure to sunlight. According to scientists, the retina of the eyes contains receptors that register the lengths of the day and night and transmit this information to the pineal gland, an endocrine organ that releases the hormone melatonin. Melatonin secretions reach their high point at night and their low point during the day.

Jet travel disrupts natural melatonin levels as we zip through different time zones. The end result of receiving more or less light is what you experience as jet lag. You may have heard of people taking melatonin supplements, or done so yourself, when flying. Curiously, left-brain types tend to find it easiest traveling east to west with the earth's energy. Right-brained types are the opposite: they feel more relaxed going west to east against the energy of the sun and atmosphere.

Circadian rhythms generally synchronize with Natural Time. The lowest body temperature occurs at about 4:30 A.M., when most of us are fast asleep. As we awaken, we experience the sharpest rise in blood pressure, the secretion of melatonin stops as the sun comes up, and a bowel movement is most likely. As this stage proceeds in midmorning, the highest testosterone levels are reached, and our bodies become more physically active at home, school, or work. By late morning and midday, we reach highest alertness and coordination. Then there is a natural lull after lunch, the traditional siesta time. In late afternoon, refreshed and reenergized, our activity picks up. Our reaction time reaches a peak, our cardiovascular efficiency and muscle strength are at their greatest, and blood pressure and temperature climax for the day. Finally, in the late evening and night, bowel movements are suppressed, melatonin secretions begin, and at 2 A.M. the deepest sleep occurs.

In traditional Far Eastern philosophy and medicine, this natural daily or circadian cycle also follows the Chi or energy flow in the meridians or streams of natural electromagnetic energy through the body. The following table shows the times when the major energetic pathways are most activated:

MERIDIAN CLOCK

3–5 A.M.: Lungs	5–7 A.M.: Large intestine
9–11 A.M.: Spleen	7–9 A.M.: Stomach
11 A.M.–1 P.M.: Heart	1–3 P.M.: Small intestine
5–7 P.M.: Kidneys	3–5 P.M.: Urinary bladder
7–9 P.M.: Pericardium/ heart governor	9–11 P.M.: Triple burner (middle three chakras or energy centers)
1–3 A.M.: Liver	11 P.M.–1 A.M.: Gallbladder

Knowing these cycles can help us tune in to our own internal rhythms. For example, breathing exercises are optimally done between 3 and 5 A.M., when the energy in the lungs is at a maximum. A bit early in the day, perhaps, but many yogis traditionally do *pranayama* and other breathing exercises at this time. Midday, from 11 A.M. to 1 P.M., when the heart meridian and its related structures, including the physical heart, the circulatory system, and the Heart chakra, are most active, is the ideal time to communicate and network with others—at meetings, at lunch, or on the phone. From 1 to 3 P.M., when the small intestine is most active, digesting and absorbing food after lunch—ideally, the main meal of the day—is the proper time for rest, study, and other quiet, reflective activities. I've grown accustomed to my listeners dozing off whenever I lecture at this time, right after lunch. I've learned not to take it personally; I sometimes find myself having trouble staying awake, too. Whether it's classes, board meetings, or athletic activities, it's better to schedule events earlier or later in the day.

From 3 to 7 P.M., when the kidney and bladder energy are at their max, is the period that is most conducive to the greatest achievement. These meridians (corresponding to the reproductive system as a whole) traditionally are held to govern will and regeneration. Most sports records, for example, are broken during this time of day, when athletes are at their peak conditioning and exhibit the greatest determination to win.

Besides jet lag, there are other conditions and disorders associated with disturbances in the circadian rhythms. These include seasonal affective disorder (the aptly named SAD), when depression strikes in the colder, darker winter months; delayed sleep-phase syndrome (DSPS); and spring migraine (coinciding with April 15, the annual IRS tax deadline).

A new science called *chronotherapy* coordinates biological rhythms with well-being, healing, and medical treatment. For example, all breast milk is not alike. Its compounds change depending on the time of day. Morning milk includes nutrients that keep the baby awake, whereas evening milk includes components that make baby sleepy. Giving breast milk pumped and bottled in the evening to a baby the next morning can make him or her drowsy and upset the natural waking and sleep cycle. Exposure to light at night has been linked to an increased risk of breast cancer. People with osteoarthritis tend to have more pain in the evening than later at night, whereas the opposite is true for sufferers of rheumatoid arthritis. For best results, treatment plans can take this into account. Similarly, eating at night, counter to the body's natural resting cycles of the kidney and bladder, can lead to overweight and obesity as the processing of food is diminished. Such findings help explain why night and late-shift workers have substantially more weight problems than their daytime counterparts. They are going against their body's natural rhythms. Of course, this understanding is not new. Healers and herbalists have known for millennia that picking a certain flower, stalk, or root in early morning, in the afternoon, or by the full moon subtly affects its taste, aroma, energy, and potency.

Another cycle that has gained a lot of contemporary attention is *ultradian rhythms,* natural rhythms that run for about an hour and a half and are repeated throughout the day. Ernest Lawrence Rossi, a scientist who has pioneered studies in this field, says that we all need to take a break for about twenty minutes every hour and a half whether we are working, studying, or playing to maintain optimal health, focus, and satisfaction. During the resting phase of the cycle, we shift from left-brain to right-brain activity. On break we are more associative, creative, and spontaneous. Many people regularly interrupt their main activity, taking periodic coffee or snack breaks, short naps, a walk, or a yoga or stretching session, or doing a crossword puzzle or brainteaser. Afterward they feel rested and renewed, ready to resume their more focused, logical, left-brain activity.

If we don't take enough breaks during the day, stress and tension build up, and we experience what Rossi calls Ultradian Stress Syndrome. USS can cause fatigue, aches and pains, and loss of memory and alertness, ultimately leading to accidents and illness. Keep this in mind when you are sitting at your desk or with your laptop for hours at a stretch!

Frequent breaks improve creativity and performance. From Leonardo da Vinci to Thomas Edison, the great artists, scientists, and inventors have discovered that after concentrated effort to solve a problem and repeated frustrations, taking a break can lead to creative insight. New ideas often pop up all by themselves. During short naps, dreams can point us in the right direction and result in eureka moments. Short breaks also reduce human error, lessen compulsive drivenness, which is similar to addictive behavior, and help us connect better with family, friends, and coworkers.

In nature, there are endless patterns of time and energy, spirals within spirals. For the most part, traditional meridian cycles, circadian and ultradian rhythms, and modern research into chronotherapy complement and support each other. The healing and medicine of the future will be increasingly based on time's harmonic ebb and flow and awareness of our internal clocks.

Embracing the Light and the Dark

Due to the ever-changing climate and environment, light and darkness, diet, social and cultural effects, and other factors, our biological clock is in constant flux and our circadian rhythms are thrown off. Happily, there are a variety of exercises and techniques to help reset your body's clock and synchronize it with your circadian rhythms. As a rule, they make use of light, sound (such as birdsong), and other natural energies and vibrations.

For example, you can awaken early with the sun by positioning your sleeping surface so that the sun will strike it at a slightly different angle as the seasons unfold. You may even want to sleep in different rooms or parts of your house or apartment. This will break up habitual patterns and also put you in touch with nomadic traditions in which our ancestors migrated from one habitat to another over the course of the year.

To awaken without an alarm clock, simply program yourself before you go to bed. Say to yourself, "It's now 11:00 P.M. [or whenever you go to sleep] and all is well. I will now enjoy a deep, relaxing, revitalizing sleep and awaken at 7:15 A.M. [or whenever you would like to get up]." Do this for a few days, and before you know it, it will proceed like, well, clockwork.

If you are really ambitious, get up just before sunrise like Peter, my neighbor the lawyer. Taking in the first rays of the early-morning sun is a time-honored meditative practice. Face east, experience the darkness and stillness, breathe in deeply, doing the "Breathe, Smile, Relax" exercise in chapter 1 of this book, experience the dawn, and absorb the energy of the rising sun. Japan is called the Land of the Rising Sun for good reason. It faces east toward the Pacific Ocean, whose vast breadth and depth magnify this energy. Shinto, Zen, and other Japanese spiritual traditions all recommend early-morning sun rituals and teach that practitioners, like the proverbial early bird, enjoy an added advantage, initiative, or energetic edge throughout the day.

For those who like to ponder life's most profound mysteries, deepest night is traditionally regarded as the best time for meditating on the nature of the universe, the mysteries of life and death, and the paradoxes of enlightenment. At about 2 A.M., the atmospheric energy for the entire day changes from yang to yin, and consequently there is a sudden expansion of consciousness during the next couple of hours. This is the complementary opposite to roughly 2 P.M., when the energy changes from rising yin to falling yang and there is a sudden sinking or diminution of consciousness, and everyone in the lecture hall seems to be fast asleep.

Nighttime, as Ray Charles sang, is the right time—for many things, sacred and profane. From sleep to sex, from dreaming to meditation, darkness is queen. Many great discoveries and inventions came to someone during the wee hours, whether awake or asleep. Friedrich August Kekulé von Stradonitz's breakthrough discovery of the benzene molecule came when he dreamed of a snake seizing hold of its own tail. Elias Howe visualized the sewing machine in a dream, and the tune for "Yesterday" came to Beatle Paul McCartney while in the land of nod. Thomas Edison—inventor of the lightbulb, the phonograph, and movies—was a night owl, typically working through the New Jersey night and catnapping during the day.

In contrast to sun time, most traditional societies based their calendars on the moon. Each month—a word that comes from the word *moon*, or period lasting between twenty-eight and twenty-nine days—was generally divided into four parts, corresponding to the phases of the moon. The new moon marked the beginning of a roughly four-week energy cycle and the full moon its peak. The first quarter of the moon was ideal for planting seeds, laying the foundation for a dwelling, and starting on a journey. It was a time of spontaneity and adventure. The second quarter of the moon was a period of heightened activity, meeting challenges, and advancing toward the goal. The full moon was the time for peak activity, celebration, feasting, public acclaim, and spiritual illumination. The third quarter was a time of harvest, completing things, and weeding out old growth and unproductive thoughts and habits. The fourth quarter, the quietest of all, was a time for prayer, meditation, fasting, and planning for the future.

In world mythology, the Moon Goddess or Queen of Night has many names and appears in many forms. Cultivating the fertile darkness of the unknown and mysterious is as much an art as opening ourselves to the light, and can be equally productive. In fact, shadows are nothing but light. For a balanced, well-rounded life, we need to embrace and integrate into our biorhythms the light and the dark, the enlightened and the benighted, as well as everything in between. And we need to acknowledge, respect, or naturally work around our individual differences in energy throughout the day.

Performing Optimally

Few of us are true night owls and fewer still are larks, whose highest energy is felt at dawn. Most of us are hummingbirds, rising to our activities as we need to throughout the day. We are, even the night owls among us, daytime creatures. Unlike our pet cats, we do not have eyes that adjust to allow us to see in the dark. Remember that workers on the graveyard shift gain weight easily. They may be awake and active, but their circadian rhythms know better, operating on hardwired instructions to slow down the body for the night.

Nonetheless, within our hummingbird status we all have different times of day that we find optimal for eating, exercising, working, making love, meditating, writing in a journal, and doing pretty much everything else we do with our days. We can't always accommodate those patterns (or teenagers would not have to start high school classes until at least noon!), and they change during different periods of our lives, but we feel better when we understand and honor our own natural rhythms. After all, they govern everything—from when we're in a good mood to when we have the highest and lowest body temperature and heart rate of the day, to when we feel most productive, to when we get our most refreshing sleep.

There are some simple techniques you can try if you'd like to train your hummingbird to fly a little differently. For example, many older people find themselves falling asleep very early and then find themselves wide awake in the middle of the night, ready to begin their day. If that describes you, be sure to spend time out of doors in the afternoon or early evening, which can reset your internal clock. In the early evening, instead of watching TV or reading, do some stretches, go for a walk, or socialize with friends. These activities will all help keep you alert so you won't fall into a deep sleep by 8:30 P.M. Blackout curtains can help, too. They tell your brain it's nighttime and keep the rising sun from prematurely signaling the start of your day.

For those who have a hard time getting up in the morning, do the opposite: sleep with your curtains open so the daylight will awaken you naturally—so much nicer than waking up to a blaring alarm that sets your heart racing. (But you'd better set that alarm as a backup!) Walking outside soon after you wake, or at least sitting by a sunny window for a few minutes, will help you feel alert all morning. The hardest technique for naturally late risers is to get up on the weekends at the same time they do during the week, but it deepens the body's sense that this is a natural cycle. The time before bed can be devoted to reading, prayer, meditation, or listening to music, not stimulating activities like watching the ubiquitous crime dramas on TV. Add a small healthy snack or glass of apple juice to punctuate the routine, and your body will begin to recognize the signals that it's time for bed.

Aligning Your Chakras

From before the time of Buddha, it was taught by yogis in ancient India that the human organism includes seven major energy centers or chakras (from the Sanskrit for "wheel" or "nexus"). They are aligned vertically along the spinal column from the Crown chakra at the top of the head to the Root chakra at the base of the spine and are ranked something like an inner totem pole. The other five are the Third Eye (near the pineal gland in the brain); the Throat chakra; the Heart or Solar Plexus chakra (near the sternum); the Navel chakra, or *Hara* (the deep intestinal center below the navel); and the Genital chakra.

The chakras are spirals (there's the spiral shape at work again) or vortices of Chi, a subtle natural life energy. They are the body's seven primary energetic clocks or gearlike wheels that control our inner rhythms and cycles. They in turn give rise to the meridians, or streams and pathways of Chi that spiral throughout the body—the organs, tissues, and cells. The

Chi flowing through our bodies governs all our physical, mental, emotional, and spiritual activities. It is nourished and affected by our external environment, the food we eat, and our thoughts, intentions, and emotions. Hence, mindful breathing, martial arts, sports, meditation, prayer, visualization, dancing, singing, listening to music, and other contemplative arts can have a profound effect on our well-being at all levels.

Like time itself, the energy moving through the chakras can flow smoothly, speed up or slow down, or be obstructed. Traditionally, health was defined as balanced Chi flow. (In Japan, the word for health, *genki*, means good [*gen*] Ki [or Chi] energy.) Health equals balance and harmony, the natural state of original being; illness implies imbalance, disharmony, and is an aberration to be rectified.

Chi or Ki energy, used in acupuncture and similar healing arts, is not routinely recognized by Western science, but it can be easily demonstrated. Hold a pendulum (or a small crystal, or even a metal nail clipper) with a thread about six inches long attached to the end several inches over the back of a person's head (ideally, over the hair spiral). Hold the string from above with one hand, and with the other hand steady it at the bottom so the pendulum stands still. Then remove the bottom hand and observe what happens.

The pendulum will start to vibrate slightly and then gradually move in a spiral. In a male, it will typically move in a counterclockwise direction. In a female, it will move clockwise. This reflects the polarity between the sexes. Man is slightly more yang than woman and proportionately more governed by heaven's downward, inward-moving, centripetal force. Woman is slightly more yin and is shaped and influenced by the earth's upward, outward-moving, centrifugal force. This helps explains many things, such as why in general women tend to talk, shop, and emote more than men do (all right-brain, associative, upward- and outward-directed activities), whereas men tend to use fewer words, zero in on what they need rather than browse or shop, and hold their emotions in (all left-brained, focused, inward- and downward-directed pursuits).

If you have two people of opposite sexes to experiment with, ask them to stand next to each other. First demonstrate how the Chi spirals differently when you hold the pendulum over each one's head. Then ask them to hold hands and repeat the test. Surprise! The pendulum stops moving. Why? Because there is now balance: Yin and yang are in harmony. Congratulations, you have stopped time. You have demonstrated the simple, age-old wisdom about energy and matter, mind and body.

With this simple low-tech tool or compass, you can discover many marvelous things. Try holding it over the other chakras. Try it over animals and plants. Try it again over a person's head, having that person visualize one by one the whole spectrum of human emotions—from greed, anger, and violent rage to love, compassion, and peace—and see how the pendulum changes. With practice, you can discover which chakras certain thoughts and feelings are coming from and even where your energy (and therefore attention) is arrested. What you envision as love may not be coming from the heart at all. And what you think of as the seat of intellect and reason may not vibrate in your head but in your solar plexus. This is the fascinating mind–body connection in action.

The chakras are your very own seven-jewel watch that enables you to keep time and balance. The chakras provide high accuracy, good temperature stability, and the ability to operate in any environment; they require little maintenance beyond clean air, healthy food, proper activity and rest, and positive, uplifting thoughts and feelings. They are known for their highly consistent precision. Unleash their internal subtle energies, untie the knots and kinks in your psyche, and unblock your channels.

To align your chakras and harmonize your subtle internal energies, simply stand straight and tall, natural and at ease like a tree. Breathe regularly, letting the gentle tide of breath rise and fall, come and go, arise and recede, and the space of your own conscious awareness, too, will settle and find its own relaxed, natural state. Let the clarity of natural mind arise from within as the snowflakes of thoughts, feelings, and concepts settle. Let everything fall into place, wherever it has to, just as it is. Breathe from your *Hara,* the Navel chakra.

Alternate breathing—from one nostril and then from the other—is another powerful way to trigger deep relaxation and help clear the *nadi,* or subtle energy channels in the body. It's connected to our ultradian rhythms. When we breathe through the left nostril, it has a calming effect; through the right, energizing. Modern medical journals have published many studies of the beneficial effects of alternate nostril breathing, showing it to increase cognitive performance, alleviate headaches and anxiety, relax both body and mind, and balance the hemispheres of the brain. The mindful attention needed to practice alternate breathing also has its benefits.

The fallout from not making peace with time in our busy lives can take the form of restlessness, sleep problems, anxiety, and other ills. Doing the following alternate nostril breathing exercise for at least twelve minutes, two or three times a day, for one to two months has been shown to have a profound effect on the central nervous system. This simple, effective technique helps relax an out-of-sync body and calm a racing mind. It's a mind-clearing, heart-opening, and energy-unblocking tune-up.

MINDFUL MOMENTS

Alternate Nostril Breathing

Sit down, relax, and come into an awareness of breathing. Let yourself settle and center in the middle of your body. Now inhale deeply through both nostrils, filling your belly, while really feeling it;

and gently, slowly, mindfully raise your left hand and close your left nostril with your left forefinger. Breathe strongly and completely out through the right nostril, entirely emptying the right side of your body—the masculine or solar *nadi*.

Then breathe in deeply, fill up, feel it again in your belly, and mindfully mirror the process, this time with your right forefinger closing your right nostril and emptying your left side, exhaling vigorously through your left nostril—the feminine or lunar *nadi*.

Then inhale deeply and breathe vigorously out through both nostrils, as well as through your fingertips, toes, and every pore of your body, letting go completely with a huge sigh of relief and exhilaration. Repeat three or seven times for full effect.

Listening to Your Innermost Heart

I have seen miracles during my twenty years in the Himalayas and India. Undoubtedly, the greatest miracle is unconditional love. What greater way can we be in sync with another? A steady spiritual practice can help us give and receive unconditional love, and along the way we will be developing ourselves mentally, physically, emotionally, and psychically. Meditation helps us to be better listeners and to exhibit greater patience, forbearance, empathy, and forgiveness. This vastly enhances our emotional and spiritual intelligence and sensitivity, improving all forms of communication and relationship. Getting in sync with others causes interactions to flow more smoothly, easing our relationship with time as we encounter less resistance and struggle.

To discover our inner rhythm and open our hearts, our most precious timepiece, we need to be willing first to make friends with ourselves and cultivate a gentle and more accepting attitude. To practice compassion or lovingkindness meditation (known as *metta* practice in the Buddhist wisdom tradition), begin generating generous, well-wishing thoughts toward your-self, without trying to change or improve anything. Make friends with your-self first, and realize a benevolent form of self-love, acceptance, and joy. Then begin to spread those warm feelings of loving-kindness to others, in ever-widening spirals of grace. This extended contentment greatly reduces the wear and tear of inner conflict and stress upon minds and bodies.

This kind of mind training or attitude transformation can help us learn a great lesson from our difficulties, instead of just trying to get past them, keep going, and survive. We can turn our stumbling blocks into stepping-stones on the path of conscious growth and inner development. Where would we be without our wounds; where would our power of com-passion, empathy, and understanding come from? In the course of time, we all experience karma, or consequences of our actions; but even bad karma can help us become more sensitive to the plight of others and contribute to their well-being. At the very least, it can help us relate to the pain and suf-fering of others, which strengthens our altruism and our humility.

I have personally found that the most painful of life's experiences often lead to the most growth, if viewed with insightful wisdom and an open, compassionate spirit. One of my favorite Buddhist *paramitas* (vir-tues or ideal qualities) is Patient Forbearance, also known as Courageous Acceptance; it helps me befriend all the aspects of myself and various facets of life, both pleasurable and painful, wanted and unwanted. Cultivating this inner strength within my own heart and mind brings indescribable peace, balance, and harmony into my life and all my relationships, and provides a still center within. Buddha taught that Patient Forbearance is the antidote to anger and violence, and that no one can make us angry if we don't have seeds of anger in our own heart. Michelangelo said that "genius is infinite patience." Patience is truly the virtue to cultivate for making peace with time and change.

The other five *paramitas* to practice and develop are Unstinting Generosity, Moral Self-Discipline, Concentrated Mindfulness, Discriminating Wisdom, and Joyous Enthusiasm. These virtues are like a reliable compass in our chaotic world and can help us navigate all of life's peaks and valleys. They allow us to skillfully cope with all manner of disappointments, sorrows, and suffering, as well as take delight in the world's abundant joys. It is how we relate to these experiences that makes all the difference. Timeless wisdom tells us that it is not what happens to us but how we respond that determines our character and our destiny.

This chapter helped you get in touch with your own internal rhythms and reconnect with the finely tuned biological and spiritual clocks inside yourself. The more you understand and connect with these rhythms and cycles, the deeper you can go into the present moment and experience its richness, subtlety, and promise.

In the next chapter, you will see that time is in the mind. Coincidences and seemingly psychic abilities are manifestations of our precious powers of perception. Aging is a state of mind that meditative practices can help slow down. As time slows and your awareness expands, you will be amazed at the gifts your enhanced perception will bring you.

CHAPTER

4

Understanding Our Powers of Perception

What is below is like that which is above,
and what is above is like that which is below,
to accomplish the miracles of one thing.

—The Emerald Tablet of Hermes Trismegistus

CYNTHIA—A PROFESSIONAL WRITER, LONGTIME student of mine, and dear friend—was recently struggling with a book deadline. She was getting to the finish line and working frantically on the manuscript's conclusion, which was due on her editor's desk by the end of that day. Feeling blocked because of her high standards and stifled by a keen awareness of how little time was left, she recounted to me how she was hunched over her computer, typing furiously with one eye on the clock, when suddenly there was a knock at her door.

To her surprise, it was Justine and Elyse, the women who clean her house every other Thursday. Since it was a Tuesday, Cynthia felt confused.

Had she been so immersed in her project that she'd lost track of the days and missed her deadline?

With a mystified smile she said half jokingly, "Today's not Thursday, is it?"

"Oh, no," Justine said. "We were in the neighborhood and just wanted to drop something off for you." She handed Cynthia a small shopping bag, with a card.

When Cynthia opened the envelope, she saw that the card was dated September 21—the all-important deadline date that had been imprinted on her brain and oppressively looming for many months.

Cynthia looked up in amazement. "How in the world did you two know that this is an important day for me?"

Justine looked momentarily startled herself. "We didn't. Is it your birthday?"

"No, it's just a big deadline. Maybe you've noticed I've been in a frenzy for the last month."

"Well, we did notice you seem to be more stressed out than usual lately," Justine replied. She and Elyse exchanged glances. "But we didn't know about the deadline. Sounds like good timing."

All three women smiled at the coincidence.

Cynthia looked back down at the card. It read: "Cynthia, Sometimes we feel alone but we are not . . . and that is a promise to us. You are a brave and strong woman, and not many people could do all that you do. BE PROUD OF YOURSELF! Justine and Elyse."

Cynthia felt moved to tears, and was almost speechless. "You two are absolute angels, and I can't thank you enough."

"You're welcome. We just wanted to brighten your day. Good luck with your deadline, Cynthia." And they walked out through the crisp fall leaves to their car and drove off.

Back at her writing desk, Cynthia opened the shopping bag, reached past the tissue paper, and pulled out a book entitled *Visions of God: Four Medieval Mystics and Their Writings,* by Karen Armstrong. She had always admired that author, and the book was on religion and mysticism—the very topic she was now working on. How could they have known?

There was more still. She reached in and pulled out a tiny pumpkin, which made her smile. And there was even more: at the very bottom of the shopping bag was a beautiful vintage blouse. It was blue green, diaphanous, and embellished with silver threads and tiny iridescent beads. It was Cynthia's favorite color, and so exquisite that she could not resist trying it on immediately. It fit perfectly.

Stunned by the perfection of the gifts, the timing, and the unexpected kindness and empathetic understanding the women conveyed, Cynthia felt an expansion, elevation, and release. All her fears and worries vanished. She returned to her computer and was able to fully focus on her work "as if I had all the time in the world." When she calmly finished her manuscript that afternoon, she was able to e-mail it to her editor right on schedule, in a relaxed, stress-free state. She had released her anxiety and centered herself in the moment, entering into Buddha Standard Time.

The Gift of the Present

One of the things I love most about Cynthia's story is how it illustrates that time is truly in the mind. I've thought about the gift of grace that these two bodhisattvas—altruistic angels, spiritual awakeners, Buddhas-to-be—gave Cynthia, which brought her back into the present moment so that she could complete her work on time. It was a gift of loving-kindness, as we Buddhists would call it. It was an unconditional present, and its timing was impeccable.

I do not know the two bodhisattvas, but I know that they were responding intuitively to Cynthia's needs. As a writer, and a highly self-critical one at that, she felt isolated and lonely. She had recently broken up with a longtime boyfriend. I knew she'd had a tough childhood with a critical and abusive father who frightened her and withheld love. As I thought about this, I felt a wave of compassion for fathers and daughters everywhere.

Cynthia was trying to let go of her past and had told me how profound she found nowness-awareness to be. As I'd reminded her, it is never too late to have a happy childhood! She was learning to experience every moment as a new opportunity to take a breath and as an invitation to start again, refreshed, renewed, and enlivened. Justine and Elyse gave her an opportunity to experience that powerful sense and use it to relieve the burden of stress that might have kept her from meeting her deadline.

It would be easy to conclude that the helpful friends were psychic. We Buddhists know that as the result of a serious spiritual practice and meditation, perception can be heightened to the point where it seems supernatural. These skills, known in Buddhism as *siddhis*, or higher powers, are often time related. In the West, we recognize them as aspects of the paranormal— including precognition, synchronicity, serendipity, and simultaneous or concurrent thought. Often what seems to be a "psychic" phenomenon is in fact the brain processing things rapidly, employing hyperfast analytical and deductive reasoning and observation, like my childhood hero Sherlock Holmes. The more mindful we become, the greater our focus and powers of observation and deduction.

Perhaps it was their Holmesian powers of perception that consciously or unconsciously allowed Justine and Elyse to discern, as they dusted her bookshelves, the type of books Cynthia enjoyed reading, and also to take note of the colors she liked. Did they notice that the boyfriend's toothbrush and slippers were no longer there? Housekeepers intimately enter our lives and tend to know all. Their appearance with that gift bag on that particular day could have been a coincidence, or it could have been a demonstration of psychic awareness. Or both. Or neither. Does it matter? All blessings and grace-full deliveries are welcome.

As you ease into Buddha Standard Time through the intentional practice of mindful meditation and present awareness, you will likely find that, along with synchronicities and serendipitous coincidences, capabilities such as mindful mind-reading, recognizing signs and omens in nature and dreams, foretelling the future, intuiting the past, and heightened powers of perception and observation in the present increase in your own life. Or, it could simply be that once your awareness expands, you take more careful notice of those innate capacities. It's not important to label our abilities. What's important is to learn to develop and use them in every moment to most skillfully deal with life, to live well and joyously, and to serve and help others.

The most powerful thing that struck me about Cynthia's story was the generous compassion, empathy, and loving-kindness extended by Justine and Elyse. In my time in India and the Himalayas I witnessed many miracles, but among all of them I would say that the greatest was the power of unconditional love. Think about the times that you've experienced an angel, or bodhisattva—a no-strings-attached benefactor or protector—in your own life and how much it meant to you. And think about the times that you yourself have been a guardian spirit to others, lending a sympathetic ear and giving them the gift of compassion at a time of need.

As Vietnamese Zen master Thich Nhat Hanh said, "The greatest gift we can offer is our presence." Think how wonderful it feels for someone to give you their full attention and for you to be truly heard, seen, and felt, and treated with kindness and care. All too often in our rushed and busy days we do not fully focus on others or remain alert to their needs. We skitter over the surface of life's waters, rarely if ever immersing ourselves in its depths. True relationship and intimacy are possible only in the present because they require genuine contact and connection, which take place nowhere but in the present moment of nowness.

When we ground ourselves in the present moment, we spontaneously connect better with others. We become more responsive and less reactive, listening more deeply and speaking with greater clarity. We gracefully step into a new zone, from mere doing to being, from listening to hearing, from reacting to responding, from imbalance to harmonious balance, from fragmentation to integration, and from separation to oneness. Through transforming ourselves, we transform all our relationships and bring the wholeness of who we are to everything we do—at home, at work, and at play. This is the miracle of relational mindfulness.

Empathic compassion, along with mindfulness and nowness-awareness, is one of the essential tools for dealing skillfully with time. Friendly and appreciative loving-kindness is the lubricant that keeps the clockwork of community running smoothly. As physics proves, the less resistance we encounter, the more velocity we generate. With reduced conflict we reach our destination sooner and have a smoother ride. This is an important lesson to apply to our interactions with others and with time.

We also achieve more velocity when we're carrying less weight. Feeling compassion for ourselves allows us to let go of our own habitual overlay and old psychological stories—excess baggage that weighs us down. We can truly begin anew in every moment with a fresh breath. As the science of neuroplasticity confirms, each new experience generates new brain cells and rewires the brain. As our neural connections are transformed and strengthened, we are constantly in the process of reshaping ourselves and our lives.

Contemporary neuroresearch suggests that cultivating compassion, kindness, and altruism through meditation influences regions in the brain that govern empathy. Recent studies involving functional magnetic resonance imaging (fMRI) have shown that loving-kindness, compassion, altruism, and other positive feelings can be learned and eventually mastered in the same way as proficiency in sports, music, art, or any other area of development.

Having compassion for others can strengthen our understanding and patience. As Plato said, "Be kind, for everyone you meet is fighting a hard battle." You often have no way of knowing the mind-set of the person who annoys you or wastes your time, or what their own personal context or psychological conditioning is. If you've been cut off in traffic, for example, perhaps the perpetrator just received devastating medical news about a loved one and is understandably upset and preoccupied while racing to the hospital. Getting angry is in many cases a waste of time and energy. Irritation can spiral, and anger can ignite like kindling and spread dangerously. We can observe our feelings, acknowledge them, and then release them without doing harm to others or ourselves. Instead of mindlessly reacting, we can mindfully take whatever steps are needed to protect ourselves. Defusing and reducing conflict greatly eases all interactions with other people and is ultimately a great time and energy saver. Sometimes it helps to pause and say a simple prayer. A learned rabbi friend, Marc Gafni, told me that when he becomes irritated or exasperated by others, he prays, "God send me patience—now!"

Mindful Manners

In these hurried and harried times it is especially important to remain aware of others, take a moment to acknowledge them in our daily interactions, and offer help when needed. Remember to mindfully give thanks, apologize, take notice, and offer acknowledgment and praise. It is a form of focus and attention. After a long line at a busy deli, when you finally receive your bagel or sandwich, do you remember to smile at the person behind the counter and give a quick thanks? With intention and focus, this small but significant act is a benediction that spreads loving-kindness. The mindful person is aware of his or her own emotional energy and can skillfully direct it for the good of all. Use your energy sagely; you will be rewarded, both now and later.

I'm reminded of an experience I had back in the mid-1970s. I was traveling by train to a Sufi center called Beshara, a farm outside London. An elderly lady with an oversize shopping bag came into the car, giving me a brilliant smile as I moved my pack over and helped her sit down next to me. "You have a lovely smile, young chap," she said, "Thank you, ma'am," I replied. "A smile is free, costs nothing, and delights everyone," she continued. "It's the shortest distance between two people. I give my smile away all day, and never run out, for I am greeted by just as many."

I was suddenly alert, realizing I had just been given a delicious gift. I thought of the many teaching tales I'd heard or read, where a spiritual master suddenly appears before the seeker to test, to probe, to remind, and to teach. Maybe this smiling traveler was really my late guru Neem Karoli Baba, dead for two years in India, famous for his tricksterism and magical appearances!

Meanwhile, the gray-haired woman just beamed at me. We hardly spoke the rest of the way, just enjoyed sitting there together while we sped by the flat green British countryside. I've never forgotten this spontaneous lesson in the Zen of smiling. Since then, I have adopted that practice of giving a smile freely and often, every day, and it has served me well. It is the positive energy and attention behind the smile that makes it so potent, and such a gift. It is a form of blessing.

Studies on Good Samaritan behavior have found that people in a hurry are less likely to offer aid to others. (Ironically, a study demonstrated that even clerics, in a hurry to give a lecture on the parable of the Good Samaritan, could literally step over someone in trouble on their way to the lecture hall.)

One study indicated that in the busiest, most fast-paced modern American cities, people were the least likely to stop in the street and exhibit basic helping behavior, whereas slower-paced cities, such as those in the South and Southwest, exhibited more such altruism. It's been theorized that cognition narrows through making haste, and also that as the speed of life increases, ethics become a luxury. As Rumi, the sublime Persian poet and mystic, wrote, "Come out of the circle of time and into the circle of love."

The more we raise our consciousness, the more we become aware of our own energy and the energy of others. Attention is a form of energy. Think about how the driver in another car looks over and glances at you when he senses you looking at him. Think about the absence of energy, for example, when you become aware that the person you're speaking to on the phone is not paying attention because he or she is multitasking (as so many of us do in our busy days). You feel their energy fade away and their focus move elsewhere. It is palpable even before you hear the clicking of a keyboard.

Enlightened Multitasking

Multitasking to me is a kind of *siddhi,* or higher power. I generally recommend that only enlightened masters attempt it. Like a Dancing Shiva with multiple hands and feet, you need to have a highly evolved consciousness to do it well. But like it or not, it is something that we all find ourselves doing at one time or another, even though for most of us it is hard enough to focus mindfully on one thing. When we multitask, we think we are saving time, but actually we are doing one thing to the detriment of another, and everything suffers. Being mindful and focused is much more effective, as you'll see when you apply the lessons of living in Buddha Standard Time to your daily life.

Buddha himself said long ago that we can hold only one thought at a time, as modern neuroscientific research has corroborated. When we think we are doing two or more things simultaneously, we are actually alternating our consciousness between them at hyperspeed, because *the brain can literally focus on only one thing at a time.* Therefore, fragmentation in focus is counterproductive, and it dissipates energy. That's why when you are focused on a work project, it is a good idea to shut down your e-mail program, let the phone ring, and ignore anything else that threatens to disrupt your work. Other tasks and diversions can wait. Focus fully and prioritize skillfully; it makes a remarkable difference in what you can achieve.

Some people get into the flow of their work (for instance, artists, scientists, and writers) but can seem preoccupied and not fully present when not at work—because their work is always percolating on a mental back burner. This creates the absentminded professor phenomenon—the visionary person who constantly misplaces his or her eyeglasses or car keys and then becomes frustrated by the waste of time spent looking for them. It could be because they are so immersed in right-brain activity (looking at the big picture) that they lose sight of left-brained linear time and pedestrian details and can't see what's under their nose. It is good for people like that to focus on connecting to and awakening the left brain. And vice versa for those type-A people who are overly rational, obsessive, and punctilious. Balancing both sides is the essence of the Middle Way.

THE POWER OF POLARITIES

Homage to Manjusri, the ever-youthful
Personification of transcendental wisdom
And discriminating awareness,
Whose blazing sword of gnosis illumines us
In cutting through attachment to illusion.
Homage to Tara, the female Buddha,
the embodiment of the sacred feminine energy within us all.
May all realize it and actualize it.

Tibetan Buddhism emphasizes the sacred feminine energy and its harmonious complement to masculine energy. Many spiritual traditions—going back to the ancient alchemists with their reconciliation of opposites, and to the shaman's unification of this world and the next—demonstrate the importance of balancing and reconciling opposites. (Jesus and early Christianity focused on much the same thing, but the original message was censored and co-opted by the patriarchy, at least until the gospels of Thomas, Philip, Mary Magdalene, and Dan Brown surfaced.) Female meditational deities and archetypes, embodying the inner qualities of wisdom and enlightenment, are invoked in various ways, including mantras and prayers; creative imagination visualizations; mudras (hand gestures); yoga postures and breath and energy work; and healing and longevity practices involving the subtle chakras, meridians, and other energy channels.

Tibetan masters teach that if a female practitioner generates the precious *bodhicitta* (awakened heart-mind) and undertakes these practices, she will often attain enlightenment or spiritual development more quickly than a man. Modern medicine and psychology have found scientific evidence for women's superior mental and spiritual dexterity as well as communication skills and relational awareness. In the 1980s and '90s, brain researchers reported that women have up to four times as many connections as men between the two sides of the brain. The corpus callosum, the main "bridge" that links the left and right hemispheres, which as we've seen can be strengthened through meditation, is naturally thicker in females than in males. According to researchers, these characteristics tend to make women in general more perceptive, articulate, and verbally fluent. And because it is easier for them to see the big picture, they can be more proficient at spiritual development. By the same token, they can become more stressed and overwhelmed than men, who, because of physiological differences, excel at compartmentalizing, focusing on a specific subject or goal, and blocking out feelings and distractions.

In Tibetan Buddhism, one of the most revered male deities is Manjusri, the god or archetype of transcendental wisdom. He is the Dharma master who embodies the timeless principles of ultimate truth and guides sentient beings across the ocean of suffering to salvation and enlightenment. Tara is the female Buddha; she represents and embodies selfless enlightening activity and feminine wisdom. Her epithets and nicknames in Tibetan include the Liberator, She Who Watches Over Us All, and Swift Responder to Prayers. We can learn and develop their spiritual *siddhis* by emulating them both in any number of ways, both contemplative and in action.

MINDFUL MOMENTS

Compassion and Skillful Means

Calling on Tara

The following Tara exercise will strengthen women and help men (and more predominantly left-brain thinkers) connect better with their right brain. It will strengthen associative abilities, enable patterns and relationships to emerge, and stimulate creative, out-of-the-box solutions. It will also enhance your love, encouragement, and compassion for others.

1. Breathe deep. Smile. Relax. . . .

2. Let go of the images you have of your ordinary name, form, and self-concept—whether you see yourself as old or young, male or female, fat or thin, sick or healthy, or other time- and space-bound qualities.

3. Visualize yourself as pure light energy arising out of emptiness, out of indeterminacy, out of impermanence, out of transparency and selflessness.

4. Imagine yourself as Green Tara or White Tara: radiant like a wish-fulfilling jewel, an emerald; or white light, transparent yet vivid, like a rainbow, like bright light refracted through a crystal.

5. Imagine your Heart chakra turning clockwise, and visualize mantra syllables or key feminine qualities such as Beauty, Gentleness, and Compassion engraved on each petal of the lotus-shaped Heart chakra.

6. Envision that heart-mind energy filling the space you are in and, in ever-widening circles, spiraling out and enveloping the earth as a whole.

7. Chant *"Om taray tu-taray turi-yay swaha,"* the mantra of Tara, for several minutes.

8. Gradually return to ordinary consciousness and assume your usual name and form, while dwelling for a minute longer in calm and stillness.

9. Retaining the feeling that you are the embodiment of timeless wisdom and compassion, resume your daily activities. In this gorgeous way enact the life of a Buddha goddess. Breathe Tara in and breathe Tara out, suffusing the whole world with blessings and well-wishing benevolence.

Calling on Manjusri

This exercise will ground men and help women (and more predominantly right-brain thinkers) to connect better with their left brain. It is especially good for strengthening memory, enhancing intelligence, giving lectures, engaging in debates or sales, or writing, playing music, or mastering any other art or craft. According to Tibetan teachings, this wisdom mantra will actually make you smarter and able to process information more quickly.

1. Breathe deep. Smile. Relax. . . .

2. Erase the images you have of your ordinary self, as in the Tara exercise.

3. Visualize yourself as pure energy arising out of emptiness, out of indeterminacy, out of impermanence, out of selflessness.

4. Imagine yourself as Manjusri, whose name means "Gentle Glory," holding a lotus flower in your left hand, sitting on a blue lion, and protecting the entire world.

5. Imagine your lotus-shaped Crown chakra (located on the spiral at the top of your head) turning counterclockwise, and visualize mantra syllables or key masculine qualities such as Truth, Discriminating Judgment, and Strength engraved on each petal.

6. Envision that energy filling the space you are in and, in ever-widening circles, spiraling out and enveloping the earth as a whole.

7. Chant *"Om a ra pa tsa na dhi,"* the mantra of Manjusri, for several minutes.

8. Gradually return to ordinary consciousness and assume your usual name and form, while dwelling for a minute longer in calm and stillness.

9. Retaining the feeling that you are the embodiment of transcendental wisdom, resume your daily activities. In this powerful way enact the life of a wise Buddha-like god acting sagely in this evanescent world.

It is beneficial to visualize and identify with these divine entities; ideally, you should alternate between these exercises to keep yourself and your internal energies in balance. Manjusri is personified as youthful, as a sixteen-year-old prince, because wisdom is pure and uncorrupted, ever fresh with each new moment. Tara is known as the Instantaneous Responder of Prayers. As you become more attuned to your own energy and awareness, unifying the Tara and Manjusri energy within, you'll be able to sense what shifts are needed. You will find that the connection between your hemispheres will grow stronger and that your intuitive powers and sense of wholeness and completeness will increase.

Drawing upon all of your mental abilities, including intuition, is useful in skillfully navigating a busy life. For example, a busy executive I know tells me that when she's faced with a daunting pile of business pitches to sift through, she can often intuit which ones will be of greatest interest to her; it helps her prioritize and save time. She says it is an ability she has developed out of necessity and that she calls upon whenever she is facing an enormous amount of work. She balances her intuition with logic, and associative thought with rationality.

Visualization is an ancient, powerful, and profound low-tech technology and can be an effective way of bending time by "pre-seeing" something. Professional athletes often visualize outcomes in order to make them come true, and it's something we can all do. The real secret is not about *things* or *goals* or what you *want,* however. How many people are there who have achieved what they think they want and still aren't happy? If you pray for what you already have, your prayers are already answered. So instead of trying to get what you think you want, the real secret is to give thanks for what you already have.

In this book I provide you with tools to help you achieve balance in your busy life of juggling obligations and opportunities. The more you practice mindfulness, meditation, and nowness-awareness, the more you will find that your vital life energy, or *prana*, or Chi is enhanced and flows more freely.

Increased energy, along with reduced psychological baggage and resistance, allows us to arrive at our destination that much more quickly and efficiently. The more our energy is allowed to flow freely, the more vitality we will have and the more heightened all our senses will become. As you will see as you continue practicing the exercises in this book, your awareness will be more refined, you will be more highly attuned, the intangible will become more tangible, and your perception and sensitivity will increase. You are training your mind through the lessons in these pages, listening to the sound between the notes, becoming aware of the space between frames, as in a film. Your consciousness is, indeed, like a movie: you can slow it down or speed it up. You are the director of your own film, your own life.

We can learn to be more perceptive of the energy of other people and animals, and tune in to the more subtle energies of everything around us, including the natural elements, colors, and metals. Mantras and other sounds such as music and chants vibrate in subtle energy centers, and further enhance our energy and unblock channels. The more freely our energy flows, the better able we are to skillfully monitor and direct it. The more balance we achieve, the better able we are to step into Buddha Standard Time—the enlightened zone in which all polarities are reconciled.

News from Shangri-La

The health benefits of living in Buddha Standard Time are manifold. In addition to strengthening the heart, lungs, liver, and other major organs, breathing exercises, mindfulness meditation, and other techniques will energize the chakras, meridians, and other pathways, and help guard against disease and disorder. Meditation increases serotonin, oxytocin, dopamine, and other neurotransmitters that contribute to feelings of joy, bliss, and well-being. It has often been noted that regular meditators seem significantly younger than their biological ages, due to increased vitality, mental flexibility, and reduced stress.

Can aging actually be reversed? Is there a way to slow down time, strengthen your mind, and even prolong your life as the years pass by? This eternal quest found literary and artistic expression in James Hilton's *Lost Horizon,* the classic novel about Shangri-La, the hidden paradise in Tibet whose members rarely get old or sick. In the Hollywood film based on the book, the residents appear youthful and dynamic even though they are several hundred years old. Though fictional, the story was based on Tibetan legends about the enlightened kingdom of Shambhala, and *Shangri-la* has entered our vocabulary as a synonym for utopia or the fountain of youth.

Is there any truth to this exotic myth? In scientific tests at Harvard, Yale, and MIT, researchers recently found that insight meditation can increase brain size and slow the aging process. To their surprise, they discovered that one area of gray matter that deals with attention and processing sensory input thickened and grew more pronounced as people who engaged in insight meditation aged. In ordinary people, this area of the cortex, or thinking cap, usually thins with age. Insight meditation does not involve chanting, thoughts, or visual imagery but focuses on bodily sensations, noises, or other sensory experience as well as paying attention to your breathing.

"Our data suggest that meditation practice can promote cortical plasticity in adults in areas important for cognitive and emotional processing and well-being," said Sara Lazar, a psychologist at Harvard Medical School and the lead investigator of the Harvard study. "These findings are consistent with other studies that demonstrated increased thickness of music areas in the brains of musicians and visual and motor areas in the brains of jugglers. In other words, the structure of an adult brain can change in response to repeated practice."

Only four of the twenty subjects were meditation or yoga teachers. The others were lawyers, health-care givers, journalists, or workers in other professions. On average the participants meditated about forty minutes a day.

In addition to improving attention and memory and slowing some aspects of cognitive aging, Lazar says, meditation can be used as a practical tool to manage your time. For example, at home or the office, people worry and get anxious about meeting deadlines or performing up to the expectations of others. "If, instead [of worrying], you focus on the present moment, on what needs to be done and what is happening right now, then much of the feeling of stress goes away," says Lazar. "Feelings become less obstructive and more motivational."

Other studies are beginning to find comparable results. At George Mason University, researchers found that several styles of Buddhist meditation could temporarily boost visuospatial abilities and improve short-term memory for minutes, and in some cases for hours. In an article in *Psychological Science*, the experimenters concluded that their finding "has many implications for therapy, treatment of memory loss, and mental training."

Meditating a few minutes every day may not enable you to live forever. But it will help strengthen your perception, memory, and focus. You may even find that you feel younger and more energetic as the years go by and that your mind and spirit continue to expand into luminous new dimensions.

Skillful breathing exercises and adroit inner practices for rejuvenation and longevity—exercises regarding the subtle *prana* body—can be found in Tibetan energy yoga, including the six yogas of Naropa. Blissful radiant inner awareness through *tummo*, a mystic–inner heat practice, has been documented by scientific researchers and found to suffuse the entire organism—on many levels, not only the physical. Vitality and energy, life force, and longevity quotient are maximized, so their reserves are fortified rather than allowed to simply wane. This is coupled with special yogic diets, fasts, ingesting sacred substances handmade for the purpose (from Himalayan herbs and trace minerals, according to semialchemical and medicinal yogic and meditational methods), mantras, prayers, and detailed visualizations.

My own late first guru, Neem Karoli Baba, in northern India, was widely reputed to be 120 years old, and Indian devotees and disciples said that he looked the same fifty years earlier as he did when I met him in 1971. When asked how old he was, he said, "Older than God." We can all strive for the realization of the deathless state, called by Buddhists the Unborn and Undying Dharma-kaya (reality-body of Buddha, or Deathless Truth). This is how we alleviate our fear of death, or how we "slay death," in ancient terms.

Another great realized master of the twentieth century, and perhaps the greatest Indian saint of the time, the widely renowned and revered sage Ramana Maharshi of South India, was always a great inspiration to me, and his small, seminal book, *Self Inquiry,* remains a minor classic of the spiritual path of enlightenment. When he was dying of cancer at an advanced age, in the 1950s, his disciples were wailing and crying and asked him not to go. "Where would I go?" the master responded to them on several occasions. He was truly beyond birth and death, coming and going. This is the real longevity or immutable realization (spiritual enlightenment) that I aspire to, not mere physical longevity from my own mortal vehicle. When his disciples asked Ramana if he would come back and be reborn to bless and protect them in the next life, he again assured them, "I am always with you. We will never be apart."

I recently had dinner with esteemed teacher Kilung Rinpoche of East Tibet, and he asked me if I was always with my *Dzogchen* master the late, great Nyoshul Khenpo Rinpoche. Without hesitation I responded that he was always with me and in me. I perceive him still. This is simply how I feel, and how I live.

Rest in the Present

Take time to sit down, or even better, curl up on your side—in bed perhaps, or on a floor rug, the grass, or a beach—close your eyes, and relax. Breathe, smile, and relax.

Let go and let be.

Let everything settle, and imagine you're like a baby, an infant, even a fetus back in the womb, free from considerations of time and place.

Rest cradled and at ease, as if floating in the warm and cozy amniotic sac of this instant, free from your habitual grown-up distractions and roles, age, gender, worries, and preoccupations.

Let the warm waters of natural awareness and nowness wash over you and through you, filling you with peace and bliss.

Know that you are held and whole, at home and loved again. Nothing else is happening.

Enjoy resting in the natural state, beyond time, beyond mind, at home and at ease in the natural great perfection of just being.

You are home now.

Go back further.

Now imagine you are dead and buried.

Enjoy that big sleep in the cool mouth of the womblike tomb,

Beyond all vicissitudes of this fleeting life.

Done is what had to be done.

Come home to yourself, your true source

And wellspring.

Breathe the light, the subtlest energy of pure being,

Beyond life and death, coming and going,

And rest in the secret inner heart of the sacred now.

With a different perception of time without limits and of how we can speed up or slow down time, depending on how fast our mind is processing the frames of experience, we can understand why aging is really about fostering our own inherited wisdom and about "paying it forward," as my young friends say. Wisdom and spiritual realization never decline, even if our mortal faculties may seem to, but grow throughout life and beyond. As my good Tibetan friend His Holiness Gyalwang Drukpa Rinpoche said recently at a speech he gave at the United Nations, "Though everything changes and is impermanent and hard to hold on to for very long, what we pass on and give to others matters very much both now and in the future, and has its own enduring magic."

We wouldn't be human if we didn't experience loss and sorrow. But as the mythologist Joseph Campbell says, "The attitude is not to withdraw from the world when you realize how horrible it is, but to realize that this horror is simply the foreground of a wonder and to come back and participate in it." We participate at our best when we are mindfully in the moment, emanating loving-kindness and compassion. It's all in our perspective and perception.

In the next chapter I'll show you practical ways to integrate mindfulness into your daily life and introduce two additional ways to enter Buddha Standard Time—through the simple, transformative arts of presencing and of meditation in action.

CHAPTER 5

Minding Time Wisely

I hear the unblown flute,
In the deep summer shadows,
Of the Temple of Suma.

—Matsuo Bashô, seventeenth-century Japanese poet

SHERLOCK HOLMES WAS ONE of my childhood heroes and a master whose lessons I still reflect on today. He was an early crime-fighting super-hero, before modern comic books, animated feature films, special effects, and video games. He worked his own magic through his refined powers of observation. His superpowers were astute reasoning based upon extraordi-narily keen observation and a perfect sense of timing. In *The Adventure of the Blanched Soldier,* Dr. Watson, his amiable but dense friend and chroni-cler, declares in admiration, "Holmes, you see everything!" And Holmes replies nonchalantly, "I see no more than you, but I have trained myself to notice what I see."

This is Right View, the first step on Buddha's noble Eightfold Path to Enlightenment, the very backbone of Buddhism. Though he's a fictional character, Holmes is as mindful and focused as they come. He always cracks the hardest cases after Scotland Yard has given up, because he's the only one who notices the river mud on someone's shoe, the mark of ladder rungs pressed onto a pants cuff, the slight crack in a suspect's eyeglasses, the condition of a workman's hands, or some other almost invisible yet telling clue. He trains himself by walking through a room, trying to capture and remember the smallest detail. Afterward, he replays in his mind what he's seen—an age-old mental memory discipline. I can't help making the parallel observation that almost every *tulku* (reincarnate lama) I know, including the Dalai Lama, had to memorize forty pages of Tibetan texts *a day* as part of their traditional Tibetan Buddhist upbringing and mind training.

Though Holmes learned the art of detection in England through his mastery of the scientific method and applied it to the world of crime, he was highly influenced by Eastern thought. In the original stories by Arthur Conan Doyle, Holmes visits Tibet incognito for two or three years, studies meditation with the high lama, and masters mindfulness and other contemplative arts. These skills, as well as his preternatural calm and detachment regarding the impermanence of life, are referred to over and over again in the stories and are, I believe, a key to his fascination to generations of readers. He's able to balance the most intense mental energy, work brilliantly with a deep inner calm and peace, and succeed in the nick of time. From Sherlock Holmes, we learn not only to be careful observers but also to cultivate mindfulness in motion, or what Buddhists call *meditation in action*.

The Great Slowdown

As a practical application of Holmes's art of detection, you no doubt know that if you want to see movement in the dark—to find someone on a dark street, for example, or an animal in the woods—you need to stand still, expanding your awareness out to the edges of your frame of vision and relaxing your gaze while remaining focused and alert. Motion and variations in light and dark will then become clearer. Similarly, when we stop our minds from constantly leapfrogging and just breathe and observe, we can easily detect greater subtleties within ourselves, as well as in others.

When our minds are still and observant, we may even begin to feel that we can read people's thoughts, since this becomes the only movement in the field of consciousness. As we saw in the last chapter, *siddhis*—or time phenomena such as precognition, coincidences, synchronicities, concurrent thought, telepathy, and so forth—are seemingly supernatural but are actually innate powers of awareness that we can access through meditational practices.

In recent years, you've no doubt heard of the Slow Movement, a populist revolt against the modern clock that promises to put us back in touch with the leisurely, natural pace of life as it has been lived for most of human existence. There's the Slow Food movement, a reaction against fast food, which originated in Italy and has now spread worldwide. Slow Foodies cook elaborate meals from scratch with the healthiest local and natural ingredients and enjoy hours of conviviality eating together. Then there is Slow Bodybuilding, a revved-down approach to muscle building that emphasizes exceedingly slow, intense lifting. Though torturous, the deliberate and focused workouts yield unsurpassed toning, energy, and vitality according to practitioners. The Slow Sex movement takes its cue from Tantra, the ancient science of the erotic arts from India and Tibet centered on prolonged but delayed gratification and the transformation of passion into compassion and bliss.

Slow Art, Film, and Lit celebrate the focused in the fine and performing arts. A prime example is Don DeLillo's novel *Point Omega,* based on *24 Hour Psycho,* a video re-creation at the Museum of Modern Art in New York of the classic Alfred Hitchcock thriller slowed down to two frames a second. It lasts an entire day. Unwinding, downsizing, and simplifying are also the object of Slow Dancing, Slow Parenting, Slow Travel, Slow Money, and similar movements.

What all these approaches enjoy in common is concentrative awareness. Buddhism has taught the beneficial art of concentration for thousands of years. Practicing concentrative meditation collects our scattered mental energies, taming our unruly minds and helping us focus and pay attention.

You have no doubt figured out that when you're struggling to remember something, often the best solution is to relax your mind. "It'll come to me," you say. And it usually does, once you stop struggling and straining. Why is that? Because everything that you have ever learned or might want to learn is at hand and available in the timeless dimension. You don't have to reach for anything. You just have to find the still center within and make yourself open to letting information come to you. Lao-tzu would probably have called this approach the way of nonaccessing. The seers of ancient India spoke of the *akashic* record—the cosmic storehouse of all and everything. It is also known as *gnosis,* from one of the Greek words for "knowledge." The psychoanalyst Carl Jung called it the *collective unconscious.* The only thing we have to do is keep ourselves and our attention in one place long enough to tap into it.

The contemplative practice of increasing focus and concentration is more about *tuning in,* creating a channel, opening the crack in the eternal moment, than it is about strenuous mental calisthenics. When we train ourselves to focus, we are really learning to be sensitive, active *receivers.* It's our number-one tool for cutting through the temporal chaos of daily life, since time itself fades away when we learn to fully focus on the present moment. When we run into trouble, we need only stop, take a breath, find our center, and take stock. Concentrative meditation trains us to do this. And the greater our level of concentrated attention, the more we can take in, the more grounded we feel, and the more able we are to make thoughtful choices.

Through contemplative awareness we learn not to let our mind—

thoughts, feelings, memories, personal narrative, and so on—get in the way of that. Here I'd like to introduce the concept of *presencing*. If concentrative meditation focuses our attention on a single point, presencing is meditation in action. It teaches us not just to live in the moment, but to intentionally, consciously, *become* the moment. If the moment is about listening, we become the essence of listening—not "a listener," but simply hearing and listening. If the moment is about engaging with someone else, we become the essence of engagement, without separation and beyond selfhood. If it's about running, we become pure motion. If it's about throwing a ball, we become the ball. If it's about fishing, we become the hunter and the hunted, the seeker and what is sought, one and the same.

Presencing takes into account our own speeds and moods. The more self-aware we become, the better we can understand how we operate and how we can attune ourselves to different conditions. For example, some people's systems seem to run too fast: they tend toward being impulsive, irritable, hyper, manic, obsessive, or anxious. Those whose systems run slow may be overly brooding types: ruminative, slow-thinking, slow to react, or depressed. Yoga, meditation, visualizations, and dietary adjustments can help people regulate and improve their metabolic rates and other speed-related systems.

So don't be afraid to mindfully slow down, to be still. As my friend Rich's ten-year-old daughter explained to him one morning as he was dragging her by the hand down the sidewalk on the way to school: "Daddy, Daddy, slow down, don't hurry! When we don't hurry, we're not late."

Masterly competitive warriors in various fields, from poker champs and magicians and yogic adepts to snipers, major-league home-run hitters, and air-traffic controllers, have had to train themselves—through constant repetition and practice—to still and seemingly stop their minds and free themselves from obscuring thoughts and emotions in any given moment. This is how they tune in utterly to a specific here-and-now instant of experience, giving them a significant edge over their opponents. Here is an experiment to help you get to that level of stillness, too.

Be Still

If you wish to cultivate absolute stillness and clarity of mind, right here and now, sit down and imagine yourself on a peaceful shore or by a tranquil lake. If the mind is a snow globe whirling with thoughts, images, memories, and inchoate feelings, then the winds of internal energy and self-seeking—analyzing, evaluating, pushing and pulling, based on likes and dislikes—are what keep it stirred up and the snowstorm in motion, obscuring the inner landscape. Let the snow globe of your heart and mind settle by relaxing, breathing deeply a few times, and releasing all the tension, preoccupations, and concerns you've been carrying—at least for the moment. Let the gentle tide of breath carry it all away like the ocean's waves, like a waterfall washing your heart, mind, and spirit clean, pure, and bright.

Now turn the spotlight, the searchlight, inward. Rest loosely and naturally in the innate state of ease and natural being. Notice the space between thoughts, beneath thoughts—the preconceptual— as everything settles and slows down and inner clarity and peace emerge from within. Rest at the origin of all things, the dawn of creation, prior to, yet ready for, whatever wishes, wants, and needs spring into being. Suppressing nothing, indulging in nothing, free from being carried away by chains of discursive thinking. Rest in it, become it, be it. Nothing more is needed.

It may take a while for you to reach this inner place of utter calm and quietude, the still center of the turning wheel of this/your universe, but let me assure you it is right there, right here, now and always.

Concentrate

If you've been trying the "Mindful Moments" exercises and the "Time Out" meditations, you understand that concentration is the key to stilling your mind, slowing down, calming down, clearing the mental fog, observing your thoughts and feelings, and ultimately minding time wisely. You're learning through the discipline of concentrated effort that you are the one in charge of your own mind, not all those distractions and unconscious drives and habits that may have been calling the shots.

In practicing basic concentration, we pay attention to one single thing for a predetermined period of time—a single object of attention, such as a word, a syllable, an image, a candle flame, the breath—to the exclusion of all else. This is the type of meditation that many of us first learned back in the '60s. Transcendental Meditation—focusing on a simple mantra for twenty minutes twice daily, in order to clear and calm the mind—was very popular at the time. People still benefit by practicing TM today. I find the candle-staring *shamatha,* or concentrative meditation, most effective, practical, and doable. Try it.

TIME OUT

Candlelight Meditation

Sit comfortably, and stare at a candle flame or low-intensity lamp. Breathe in and out, maintaining a fixed yet gentle gaze upon the light source. When the mind wanders and the attention wavers, simply notice that it is happening, without judgment or reaction. Use the leash of re-mindfulness to bring the wandering attention back to the light, and pay attention to it wholly and with single-pointed, focused intensity. Let everything else go by.

Don't become discouraged when the monkey-mind—your wandering attention—keeps leaping and bounding away, as it will.

Simply notice this distraction, this lapse in attentiveness, and again and again bring the wandering attention back to focusing single-pointedly on the flame or light. Blink as you need to.

Let the breath and mind settle.
Calmness and clarity emerge from within
and rest on this single image before you.
Look at the light,
Become the light.
Breathe into the light,
Merge with the light.
Be light.

There are many such gateways in daily life to this kind of Full Connection Meditation, those times when we are deeply drawn into an experience of sacred union. They are valuable natural resources.

Concentrative practice helps sustain and further mindfulness. As we become more able to observe and understand the why and how of our daily preoccupations and self-imposed limitations, we develop insight, wisdom, self-knowledge, and understanding. We also become more skillful and experienced in anything requiring a high degree of focus. We become better listeners, better drivers, better dancers, better performers, better lovers, and better parents, making better use of our time. The further we go into the moment—this moment, right now—savoring its breadth, depth, and richness, the richer and fuller we become as human beings.

Just how do meditation and mindfulness practices work to slow down time, subdue the emotions, and quicken joy, sympathy, calm, and other positive emotions? Since the 1930s and '40s, research has shown that the human brain produces four basic types of vibrations:

- Beta waves (13–38 hertz, the measurement of brain frequency) occur during active thinking and problem solving.

- Alpha waves (8–12 hertz) take place during relaxation and calm.

- Theta waves (4–7 hertz) correspond to sleep, deep relaxation, hypnosis, and visualization.

- Delta waves (below 4 hertz) occur during sleep.

More recently, a fifth type—gamma brain waves (39–100 hertz)—have been discovered. They are produced during higher mental activity and the consolidation of information. They are present upon awakening and during rapid eye movement (REM) sleep, as well as during higher states of awareness, including meditation.

Compared with ordinary consciousness, meditation increases alpha, beta, theta, and gamma waves and reduces delta waves. The overall effect is to increase concentration and contribute to a calm, creative, and focused pattern of brain activity. As we have seen, meditation also increases synchrony between the two hemispheres of the brain, contributing to originality, alertness, and freshness of perception.

On the Road

In the Satipatthana sutra (or scripture), the Buddha described the Four Foundations of Mindfulness. These teachings remind us to be aware of (1) our bodies, including both our posture and our physical sensations; (2) our feelings and emotions; (3) our thoughts; and (4) events and deeper patterns as they occur, moment by moment. Let's think about this Mindfulness sutra in terms of a modern problem like being stuck in traffic.

Americans spend three hours a day driving, on average. For many their time behind the wheel is one of chronic stress, tedium, and frustration. For those who commute to work, gridlock, close calls, and fender benders can become a way of life. Even driving to a nearby grocery store can be a challenge: the vast majority of accidents happen near home, on familiar, well-traveled roadways. Driving while texting is fast displacing driving while drunk as the major cause of accidents.

Imagine you are one of these harried drivers, stuck in traffic yet again—surely one of the most frustrating situations where you feel that your time is being wasted. If you can shift your attention away from feeling powerless and trapped, you will be able to see the situation as an opportunity for mindful meditation and a very different way of experiencing the moment. For this is a classic state of *bardo*, a Tibetan word meaning an in-between state, as between death and rebirth, or between one thought and another. It is an opportunity for inner work, awakening, and transformation.

Begin by bringing your attention to every detail, moment by moment. Instead of wishing you were somewhere else, observe the cars around you, the stopping and starting of the traffic pattern, the smell of the summer air coming in your window or of your heater as it keeps you warm in the winter, and the state of your own mood as well. Notice that you are actually sitting in your car and not just "going somewhere." Feel the sensation of the seat upon your thighs and buttocks. Notice whether your body feels hungry, stiff, tense, anxious, or relaxed. Notice whether you're upset about being stuck in gridlock, whether you're anxious about other parts of your life, whether you feel alert or sleepy. Notice the itch on your nose and the way your toes feel in your shoes. Notice the details of the people in the cars around you—whether they seem happy, bored, preoccupied, or calm.

Notice the sunny or cloudy day, the sounds of the cars inching forward, the traffic copter whirring overhead, maybe the chirp of a bird. Notice the stream of thoughts and emotions going through you as you observe the changing scene around you. Notice whether you are impatient and angry about the sheer waste of time, and notice what other drivers and passengers seem to be feeling. Notice whether you feel sympathy toward them (misery loves company) or resentment, envy, pity, or some other emotion. Notice whether your sympathy, understanding, and compassion grow or diminish as you slip effortlessly into Full Connection Meditation.

Notice with an alert and vigilant mind, yet try to remain unattached to any of it. It's all small stuff, and there's no need to sweat it, as the saying goes. It's merely the flotsam and jetsam of raw, unmediated experience. Let it go; let it all come and go.

Notice the larger stuff: the trajectory of your life; the long, winding road of time. Imagine what kind of insight could turn the experience of sitting in traffic, right here and now, into one of the most memorable moments in your life.

And guess what? While you have occupied your mind with noticing all these things, time has slowed and even disappeared. You feel calm and grounded. You have gracefully accepted things as they are. Perhaps you even avoided being in an accident by staying put for that time period. Most important, you have used the opportunity to be meaningfully engaged in what you are doing. You have turned from vegetating to meditating.

Every moment, every minute, every hour, day, or night gives you such an opportunity. If we can reflect upon this continuous flow of impermanence in our lives, we can loosen the tight grip that our ideas and fixations have upon us and flow more easily with the dreamlike, somewhat insubstantial, yet miraculous nature of how things actually are. Traffic flows or stops flowing. Everything is transitory, and neither state will last.

I have another traffic story that illustrates the benefits of minding time wisely. I was trying to get to my writing studio one hot summer day, and the traffic had slowed to a crawl. I was anxious, thinking about my to-do list, but then I decided to drop into a more productive place in myself.

I began simply noticing. I noticed that my whole right leg and foot felt tense on the pedals. I noticed how my hands were gripping the steering wheel, and I asked myself where all of that tension came from. It suddenly hit me: those were my mother's hands gripping and her voice inside my head. I remembered how when I was a child, she would always worry about being late, pushing and trying to get the most out of everything. That attitude wasn't me at all, but had become a little habitual voice inside my head.

So I said to myself, "Relax, Mom!" I took a few deep breaths, my shoulders dropped, and I got back into balance. I sat in the car while driving instead of whipping myself forward like a racehorse trying to get to the finish line. A wave of compassion for my mother (and myself), as well as for all parents and children, washed over me in that instant. I forgot who I was, where I was, and where I was going. Releasing all of myself, I came back into myself. And when I got to the studio, I had an especially productive session.

Right Driving might be a modern adaptation of Buddha's exhortation to Right Mindfulness, part of his noble Eightfold Path to Enlightenment— what some commentators have called "the oldest extant successful business plan in history." The eight steps are these:

1. RIGHT VIEW: seeing things clearly just as they are

2. RIGHT INTENTIONS: understanding causation, cause and effect, and interconnectedness, impermanence, subjectivity, and unselfishness

3. RIGHT SPEECH: using words that are true, appropriate to the situation, kind, helpful, nonviolent, and conducive to the greater good

4. RIGHT ACTION: acts congruent with the basic Buddhist precepts regarding cherishing life and refraining from lying, stealing, sexual misconduct, and intoxicants that cause heedlessness

5. RIGHT LIVELIHOOD: engaging in honest, productive labor that harms no one and benefits people as well as oneself; making a life, not just a living; finding your true vocation

6. RIGHT EFFORT: balanced effort, diligence, energy, perseverance, and joyous enthusiasm

7. RIGHT MINDFULNESS: alert presence of mind and attentiveness to present-moment experience, outer and inner, without judgment or manipulation

8. RIGHT CONCENTRATION: being focused on the task at hand, giving special emphasis to what will ultimately be conducive to awakened enlightenment, spiritual freedom, inner peace, and deathless bliss.

Good spiritual business advice, indeed.

Make Haste Slowly

From the Latin admonition *Festina lente,* or "Make haste slowly," and Aesop's fable of the Tortoise and the Hare, in which "slow and steady wins the race," to jazz great Hoagy Carmichael's tip "Slow motion gets you there faster," we have long been instructed to slow down. According to Milarepa, the great eleventh-century Tibetan yogi and poet, "Hasten slowly and you will reach your destination." There are plenty of things that benefit from a slow pace, like making love, savoring a delicious meal, reading a book you enjoy, mentoring kids, and walking in nature.

But the pressure to hasten and have it done yesterday keeps accelerating. Take Tony, a thirtysomething New York criminal attorney. Whether in court, at the law library, at the gym lifting weights, or at a bar meeting women, he was always in motion. Juggling clients, court appearances, a plethora of PDAs including two smartphones, a hyperactive love life, his former frat brothers, and a baker's dozen of relatives nearby, Tony spent much of his day hurrying from one place to the next. "I wish I could clone myself," he would frequently jest. "Then maybe I'd be able to keep up!"

A crazy timetable, poor-quality food, and constant anxiety about falling behind eventually took its toll. Tony began getting panic attacks, and after he repeatedly showed up in court too fatigued (and once too hung over) to represent his client adequately, the judge held him in contempt. But rather than fine him or sentence him to Rikers Island to unwind and "do time," the judge gave him the option of enrolling in a stress-management program. Tony ended up going on a Buddhist retreat in the Catskills, where he learned to Slow Walk rather than Power Walk. This technique simply involved walking as slowly as possible to get where he was going, simply concentrating with undivided attention upon one step at a time and one breath with each step—making a few small steps toward aligning his life with his vision.

To his amazement Tony, just like my friend's daughter, found that he experienced getting where he was going more quickly than when he hurried, and he arrived clear, alert, and refreshed. In the process he discovered *psychological time,* or how his awareness and mood affected his experience of the moment. He observed how time seems to stand still while we're bored or waiting for someone, or might seem to fly by when we're immersed in an activity. This is because time is so subjective. Tony learned to be mindful of the sights, sounds, smells, and other stimuli he encountered, as well as his own breathing, thoughts, and feelings, and tuned in to his own rhythms and needs in an adaptive manner, changing his mind to change his perception of and reaction to time.

Now Tony hastens slowly, making his many rounds in Manhattan. He has a new spring in his step and a steady girlfriend for the first time in years, and he stops and feeds the pigeons during lunch. The judge was so impressed with the improvement in Tony's attitude and behavior that he went on a meditation retreat himself. Perhaps one day the contemplative arts will transform enough of us that society as a whole will feel more deliberate, calm, and peaceful.

Daily Mindfulness

Training ourselves to be highly observant, reflective, and the perfect objective witness is not easy in the beginning. Inevitably, we will lose focus and concentration. But when this happens, we need to gently remind ourselves of the object of our attention. Strengthen your re-mindfulness muscle by flexing it over and over. There is an infinite variety of experiences, both inner and outer, that we can attend to, from taking a slow, careful, mindful shower, to chewing each mouthful three to four dozen times, to observing with detachment all of the places we go to in our minds when we are unable to fall asleep. The possibilities are limited only by our imagination and dedication.

My own inspiration for these practical meditations for daily life is Saichi Asahara. I wish more people today knew about this mid-nineteenth-century Japanese Buddhist. A sandal maker and poet, he once said, of shaving off slivers of wood or leather, that with every stroke of the blade he was building Buddha's temple in the Pure Land, the abode of enlightenment. I like to remember Saichi Asahara's example of mindfulness when I'm shoveling show, washing dishes, or laying bricks for a wall or walkway—every stroke of work accomplished in awareness and in the spirit of joyful service is building a better world. This is our real work.

Mindfulness can be practiced anywhere, anytime, and by anyone. Here are some practical ways to begin.

Mindful Walking.

When you next take a walk, free yourself from your electronic friends: iPod, cell phone, or Kindle. Pay attention to everything with consciously heightened awareness: the sights, sounds, smells, the feel of your body moving ahead along the path, the feel of your feet on the earth with each step. If you find your attention wandering, stop walking and stand still, gently collecting yourself and recollecting what you're engaged in. Take a few deep breaths, and then start moving ahead again. Just walk—aerate and irrigate the brain, nourish the heart and soul—while enlivening and strengthening the body, too. Just walk, letting go of everything and practicing full engagement in only two activities: walking and breathing. You will be amazed at how quickly time passes by as you're going as slowly as you can, and how relaxed, refreshed, and present you will gradually come to feel.

Aside from sitting and chanting, walking is perhaps the best-known form of meditation. Walking meditation is a slow, contemplative walking practice or exercise in which you mindfully observe yourself lifting your feet one at a time and then placing each one down again. In a more advanced version, you synchronize your breathing with your slow, mindful walking, one step at a time—one in-breath, one footstep; one out-breath, one footstep—repeating this again and again while concentrating your attention entirely on what you are doing.

Mindful Resting.

When you lie down, whether it's outside on the grass or on a rug, couch, beach chair, bed, or futon, don't drift off immediately. Instead, intentionally cultivate attentive awareness, becoming mindful of feelings, sensations, perceptions, and thoughts while temporarily letting go of other habitual concerns and mental preoccupations. Relaxed and at ease, yet vigilantly aware, enjoy this dreamlike pose and let go of everything. And if you do drift off, you'll discover that ten minutes of sleep feels like a restful hour.

Mindful Listening.

A more subtle internal moment of directed mindfulness can be cultivated (exploited, even) during the day by any number of different little mindfulness experiments, even in the midst of other activities. For example:

- *Tune in to your hearing:* Stop, close your eyes, take a few breaths, and then relax and fall into deep listening. Become aware not only of the sounds outside, but also of the inner sounds: the beat of your heart, the pulse of blood in your ears, the soft sound of your breathing.

- *Tune in to your body:* After taking a few calming and relaxing, stress-relieving breaths, clench and unclench your fists a few times, and perhaps the soles of your feet as well, and completely relax; then gently become mindful of whatever sensations in your body seem to be dominant. Whatever they are, simply "cradle" them, letting them be as they are, without judgment or concern, but observing them with your innocent inner gaze, empty of the past and free of the future. Simply befriend yourself and all of experience with your open heart and clear mind. He who befriends himself is befriended by the whole world. When you become clear, everything becomes clearer.

If you wish to go further, listen to the sounds inside your body; become the sounds; be the sounds. Sense intuitively where the sounds are coming from. Trace back sound to its source and dissolve there, as sounds themselves recede and an empty, luminous openness beckons.

All perceptions—sights, fragrances, thoughts even—can similarly be traced back to their true source and home as we move beyond the horizon of personal experience and dissolve into the zone of pure consciousness.

Mindful Fitness.

Bicycling is one of my favorite ways to "sweat my prayers," as dance teacher Gabrielle Roth calls it. What is easier as an object of attention than simply breathing and pedaling? I do it in the winter on a recumbent stationary bike in my basement, and in the good weather outside on my blue ten-speed bicycle. Here's the secret of meditation in action: simply doing what you're doing while letting everything else go, come and go, and really—bottom line—just *be*. Paying enough attention to keep going—in this instance, pedaling and steering—and letting the rest of awareness float free and easy. Unplugged from media, letting the mind and heart settle as the spirit soars free of daily concerns and preoccupations. Just breathing, pedaling, and soaring along. Not even trying to get anywhere. Make sure to keep going through any resistances that might arise, and catch the updraft of your second wind kicking in and carrying you forward. You will be surprised at how much more energy you now have.

Mindful Communion with Animals.

Animals as a rule live in Buddha Standard Time. Being in their presence can teach us many lessons. Watch a dog leap for a Frisbee and you'll experience time slow down and come to a stop. When you spend time with an animal companion, or with birds, reptiles, bugs, and butterflies in the wild—any of God's creatures—the experience of communion can be truly soul shaking and time shattering.

As a Buddhist, I aspire to a mindful way of living, following the Eightfold Path. It can take many lifetimes to get all these wise *right*s just right. But when I used to look at my beautiful white sheepdog Chandi bounding through the woods like an exuberant, fearless child, I would think: she is *right* without even trying. She just *is*. Our pets instruct us daily, without words or lesson plans, in the meaning of the golden eternity, here and now.

Mindfulness can be applied to any activity. Beginning right now.

The Zone

Many people work best under pressure—but why? Maybe not having enough time to dillydally is a good thing. Have you ever noticed how your to-do list comes into sharp focus when you realize that finishing means that you can take a whole day off and go to the beach or a concert, movie, or sports event? There is nothing so productive, the saying goes, as waiting to do it at the last minute. Ben Franklin, that wisest of timekeepers, knew the secret of his calling. "If you want to get something done," he advised counterintuitively in *Poor Richard's Almanac,* "ask a busy man to help."

We often live most present and accounted for when we are pushed to our edge. Our senses become heightened because of deadlines or danger, or because we have become so deeply absorbed in a project that we lose all track of time. Our survival instinct, adrenaline and other enlivening hormones, and our passionate enthusiasm for our subject are aroused and further stimulated by the shock of realizing that we're on the brink of failure, danger, disaster, crisis. It is this natural reaction to danger or crisis that instinctively stimulates our energy, thoughts, and talents toward completing the work at hand and ignoring other possible distractions and diversions. No matter how long we've been procrastinating, our hormones and enthusiasm now drive us to become lost in our work. We see this in athletes all the time: the home run that saves the game, the buzzer-beating shot swishing through the basketball net.

We get in a groove, and things flow in such a way that it seems as if exactly what we need simply manifests itself. Psychologist and creativity expert Mihaly Csikszentmihalyi calls this "Flow"—the state of being when we seem to accomplish everything without effort and we know instinctively what needs to be done to reach our goals. In business and sports, it's called "peak performance," "personal best," or being "in the zone." Each of us has experienced these moments at one time or another. But how many of us know how to evoke this state of grace or flow intentionally? Our Buddha self lives in a constant state of flow. The Buddha within is always awake. It is we who are often asleep at the wheel of our lives.

People who have trained for years to become detached from fear and unthinking behavior can face a life-or-death moment and immediately know what to do. That's called having supreme presence of mind—the ability to act intelligently and quickly in a crisis.

I read in the news about a fifty-two-year-old construction worker in China named Wang Jianxin who was assigned the job of digging a ditch sixteen feet below ground. He got to work with just a shovel and a plastic safety helmet. Suddenly, a huge wall on one side of the ditch collapsed, burying him under an enormous pile of earth.

The rim of Wang's helmet trapped a tiny pocket of air near his face. Doctors later reported that he had about five minutes' worth of oxygen. A practicing Buddhist, Wang knew that fear and panic would accelerate his breathing. When he found himself in heavy blackness, he let himself drop into concentrative meditation, intentionally calming his thoughts and energy, and thus slowing down his breathing and heart rate. He trusted that eventually he would be freed, especially if he prolonged his air supply this way.

It took a crew two hours to dig him out, and they found Wang alive and conscious! The deep calm and discipline achieved through years of meditative practice saved his life.

Wang's response to his crisis was both instantaneous and automatic, a result of years of dedicated practice. Experienced meditators are trained to recognize the truth or reality as it presents itself in each moment. Wang's training had taken him to a point of absolute conviction. He knew his inner strength and that he could use his disciplined mind to concentrate on slowing his physical systems to improve his chances of survival. At the same time, such training would also prepare him to accept the possibility of a peaceful transition into death.

Such groundedness is the essence of what we call *presence,* and you can develop it, too. An individual with presence controls his or her destiny, always, even unto death.

The samurai warrior code of Zen Buddhism treats every moment as if it were a matter of life or death. If we train for life as a spiritual emergency, then we can feel a sense of urgency about paying attention, living in the here and now, and practicing what I call *cherishment*—endeavoring to treat everything and everyone as divine, unique, and extraordinary, and with gratitude and appreciation. We will know how to answer the questions that worry us: If I lose a loved one, how will I cope? If I get a chronic illness, where will I find the strength to go on? If the car goes into a spin on an icy road, will I know what to do? If the house burns down and I lose everything, will I be able to go on?

Being Fully Present

There are two practices, one formal and the other informal, that I commit myself to every day to develop my awareness and make the most of my time, energy, and potential.

First, every day I set aside a time to do a formal session of meditation. Usually it is a sitting meditation, but sometimes I meditate while walking, standing, or contemplating the garden or something in nature—especially if I'm traveling. With these practices, I am cultivating *attentive presence.* I'm not trying to formulate or create anything, imagine or visualize anything, or get anywhere.

Second, throughout the day I commit myself to responding fully to whatever needs to be done, giving 100 percent of my attention and energy as best I can, while also not doing more than is needed or wanted. When I'm in the car, I just drive and minimize any distractions.

As I give my all in these two aspects of my day, I also free myself of both of them when I am done at the end of my day. I am satisfied, and I let go and move on. This, in essence, is the sacred art and practice of presencing—integrating the clear light of being fully present into the muddy haze of daily life.

The key is complete focus and commitment to wherever your mind and heart rest. Many of us slog or speed through life in a rote, unconscious way and are not really *present* for much of it. Cultivating mindful awareness of our thoughts, feelings, and deeds, and accepting the law of karma— a balanced action and reaction—are ways to stay clear and maintain a high level of attention.

We Are Already There

When you take even a brief mindful moment for discovery, you can bring breathing space to a claustrophobic day and energize yourself with the freshness and immediacy of experience. You can practice presencing until you create your own little zone of hyperawareness. Then, when you are in this zone, you are suspended in time like a great bird soaring in flight—all-seeing, above it all, free.

Examples of presencing can be found in the Zen arts, including flower arrangement, archery, swordsmanship, haiku poetry, painting, Noh drama, the tea ceremony, gardening, and motorcycle maintenance. The preeminent Japanese medieval swordsman Musashi also practiced Zen painting, sculpture, and calligraphy in his later years. One of his works is a *sumi-e* (ink brush and paper) painting of a shrike on a branch. With only the simplest of gestures—*blop!* the bird; *swish!* the branch—there is one of God's little creatures, looking ready to fly off the page.

A student of the Zen arts will practice over and over until the preoccupied and distracted self gets out of the way and pure essence begins to flow in free, spontaneous expression. This kind of creation manifests itself without ego or effort. The accomplished Zen master needs no help, because every moment is creatively fertile, beckoning. He or she is at the dawning of creation, living in time but not bounded by its limitations.

We, too, can learn to live this way—and to truly *live* rather than simply be born, age, and die. This is the basis for the age-old teaching about treating each moment as if it were our last. This is the power of presencing. By slowing down, being more mindful, and cultivating the art of silence, we can learn to use time wisely and anchor and ground ourselves in each moment. By lightening our *selves,* we open up to ever-expanding horizons of awareness and can learn to make space for realization and transformative insight at deeper and deeper levels.

In the next chapter, we will explore further approaches to mastering time's flow, especially by expanding and contracting time according to our personal needs and desires, as well as by varying the tempo. In this next step toward living in Buddha Standard Time, you will discover a new radiance and spaciousness to life.

CHAPTER

Creating Space in the Pace

We have more possibilities available in each moment than
we realize.

—Thich Nhat Hanh

PHIL, MY REGULAR UPS deliveryman, followed the same routine every
day. He would get up while it was still dark, load his truck, and be on the
road most of the morning and early afternoon delivering packages. His
circuit was as predictable as clockwork, and he saw the same people, the
same dogs, and the same traffic congestion day after day. To compensate,
he became addicted to hip-hop, talk radio, and other audio distractions.
"The tedium was numbing," he admitted. "I was just waiting for my shift
to end each day so my real life could begin."

I suggested that Phil turn down the static and open his eyes and ears to
nature around him. I explained that instead of pushing through the tedium,
which made the day seem endless, he might try to find something in his day
that could grasp his interest. He said he'd give it a try. So he picked up some
DVDs and books on bird-watching and in short order became an avid birder.

A few months later he told me: "I get up with the birds, literally, so it was easy to take advantage of the timing. I started with the blue jay, cardinal, red-tailed hawk, and common varieties of sparrows and warblers. Recently I saw a peregrine falcon, and I was so excited when I spotted a marbled godwit that I dropped my package! Luckily it wasn't marked Fragile. I got the picture, though."

He proudly showed me a photo of the rare godwit on his cell phone, along with dozens of other photos of birds. "People don't like their UPS deliveryman taking pictures in their front yard," he acknowledged sheepishly. "But when I take out a cell, it looks like I'm just calling the home office. And, you know, in a way I am!"

Now, instead of waiting to punch out on the time clock each afternoon, Phil is contentedly shooting away, listening to birdsong, and memorizing verses from *The Conference of the Birds*, a twelfth-century Sufi classic he has grown to love. Nothing has changed about his route or the monotony of delivering packages, but with his new interest, his day has been reframed and transformed. His time has become his own.

Phil uncovered a valuable secret: if we want to make peace with time so that our days feel neither overwhelmingly rushed nor glacially slow, we need to *change the space of the pace*—wake ourselves up by doing something different that shifts us to another way of being. In this chapter you'll learn how.

Let's start by examining a big drain on our time: excessive people pleasing.

The Right Kind of Compassion

Many of us are continually bombarded with urgent demands on our time and energy from family, friends, and often neighbors, coworkers, and even strangers. For the most part, we are happy to oblige if we can fit their requests into our busy schedules and tight budgets. Bring something to the post office? Give someone a lift to the airport? "No problem," we reply cheerfully. The Golden Rule—"Do unto others as you would have them do unto you"—is not only a spiritual commandment engraved into our psyches, but also good, practical advice. The good deeds you do for others are often reciprocated. As long as both parties don't take unfair advantage, the unspoken quid pro quo works.

The problem arises when there is an imbalance between parties or someone thinks you "owe them one." When the giving becomes one-sided, it is incumbent on us to remedy the situation. Otherwise, we will cause others to suffer because of our mindlessness or we will suffer as a result of theirs. The vicious circle that can ensue leads to further resentment, anger, and misunderstandings. But there are ways to rebalance the scale when you feel you are giving too much.

MINDFUL MOMENTS

Does It Deserve Your Time?

You're not doing anyone a favor by acceding to unreasonable or frivolous demands on your time, energy, or pocketbook. Buddhists have a wonderful name for acquiescing to others' unreasonable demands: Idiot Compassion. You have to know when to say no, known in Buddhism as showing Wrathful Compassion. Sometimes you have to draw the line, but where and when? Here are some practical guidelines to cultivating space by reclaiming your time as your own:

1. Are you healthy and strong enough to do what is asked? If your physical, emotional, or spiritual health is low or inadequate to the task, that alone rules it out. If someone needs to be driven somewhere or wants you to help them move and you're feeling depleted, tell the person that you don't feel good enough, that you're sorry but you're not up to it. Similarly, if the weather makes it difficult or dangerous to do someone a favor, turn it down. Maintain healthy boundaries and expectations. Nowhere is it

written that you have to be a hero. And as we've already learned, compassion begins with yourself.

2. Is the request on your time reasonable? In other words, is it clear, concise, and limited? You don't necessarily want to commit to a vague or open-ended task like watching someone's child whenever a parent gets in a bind. Don't shy away from clarifying what specifically is involved, how long it will take, and who will pay for any expenses, such as gas.

3. Is the request petty? Now, this can get tricky, because what's petty to you may seem vital to someone else. But if you are being asked to chauffeur, shepherd, mother, or fill in for someone to enable that person to evade responsibility—for example, driving a teenager to a party so he can get drunk or stoned—then you might well decide to draw the line. This becomes an exercise in distinguishing the self from the Self, and small, ordinary, sequential time from larger cyclical or timeless Time by keeping in mind the bigger picture and long-term consequences.

If these criteria are met, then by all means give freely of your time, energy, money, support, encouragement, help, and love. But if not, step back. Find a way to give a constructive, affirmative "No thank you" in answer to the request. In the case of a child, friend, or someone else with whom you have a custodial or closely interdependent relationship, explain clearly why the proposed activity is not in your or their best interest and politely decline, perhaps adding the phrase "for now." In the case of someone who is argumentative, aggressive, or dependent, avoid disagreeable discussions that further drain your energy. Simply withdraw to an inaccessible high ground or keep a safe physical and/or emotional distance. Say yes to your Self by gently saying no to unreasonable demands and expectations.

Why let simplistic or misguided notions of compassion draw you into becoming a supporting actor or actress in someone else's soap opera or fantasy? Don't feel obliged to respond to annoying calls, e-mails, or tweets. Preserve your integrity and tranquillity. If you like, you can pray or meditate for their well-being, sending them compassionate thoughts and good energy.

When there are a lot of demands made on our attention, not only does it drain our life force, but if it involves negative or useless energy, we can actually feel weakened by the effects. In Buddhism, "leakage" is one of the translations for the word that is usually translated as "defilement"—a key concept encompassing greed, hatred, delusion, pride, and jealousy. Buddha himself diagnosed these as "the five basic poisons" that destroy our harmony, peace, integrity, and well-being. The leakages or disturbances in our energy fields obscure the rising sun of the clear light within us. It takes focus, clarity, intention, and healthy boundaries to conserve and intelligently channel our inner resources. Patient loving-kindness is one of the greatest forms of protection.

Scientists once believed that we have only a finite number of brain cells and that our attention span is limited. But a 2007 study under the direction of Richard Davidson at the University of Wisconsin in which researchers monitored subjects who meditated for three months, demonstrated a hitherto scientifically unrecognized ability in meditators to slow down, to increase their attention span markedly, and to track and focus quickly on a number of different targets. Tibetan Buddhist meditation was found to be a primary tool for conserving energy, increasing attention, and enhancing happiness.

In a crisis or emergency, a regular meditation practice—even the simple "Breathe, Smile, Relax" exercise that I showed you in chapter 1—can help us collect ourselves and reconcentrate our energy and attention. Learning how to do this prevents the cupful of golden vitality poured into us at birth from being continuously drained away. Meditating and being mindfully aware can keep the cup brimming.

Let's look at how this translates into real life. As a real-estate agent in a major metropolitan area, Karen was constantly on the go. Afraid she would miss an opportunity, she felt obliged to be always on call, even when she should have been at home taking care of her two school-age children. "I felt in thrall to my job," she explained. "I'm really good with people, but having to go out to show a property on the whim of a client became a chronic headache. And then when I'd get back, the kids or Jason, my husband, would monopolize all my energy. I had no time for myself."

In addition to basic Buddhist breathing and centering exercises, I suggested to Karen that she find a meditative space to go to in the city between her appointments. "I know just the spot," she exclaimed, brightening at my suggestion.

Several months later, when I saw her again, Karen recounted how there was a scenic spot she liked in a park in the center of the city: "There's a tiny bridge that crosses the river and a small waterfall leading to the ravine. It's one of those picture-perfect spots. But because it's off the beaten track, it's never crowded."

Not only does Karen take frequent pauses in her hectic schedule these days to visit this little oasis of peace and tranquillity, but she also brings some clients there. "By refreshing me, it has actually made more productive use of my time," she said. "Just the other day, the couple I was with were torn about living in the city or the country. But after I took them to my special place, only ten minutes from the condo I was showing, they decided to take it on the spot."

It's amazing what good can come from slowing yourself down and paying attention. Think of little respites you can give yourself—time within time—as Karen did, to help you see things clearly and connect more strongly with nature and with other people.

The Art and Science of Waiting in Line

Many of us feel that daily life is a race against the clock, made even more stressful by the constant interruptions, delays, obstacles, and unforeseen events that cut into our busy schedules. When we run up against situations like these, life becomes *too slow*.

How can we deal mindfully with waiting in long lines at the bank, the restaurant, the grocery store, or the doctor's office? What can we do when the automated response puts us on hold? When the weather turns bad and all flights at the airport are delayed or cancelled? Businesses and individuals have come up with some creative ways to keep time from feeling interminable.

In the former Soviet Union, people had to stand in line for hours to buy everything from a toothbrush to a television set. There was commonly one line to pay for it, one to get a clerk to put in a request to inventory, and another to have it delivered to you. Many took advantage of the downtime to read novels, poetry, or art history texts. As a result, Russians as a group are extremely cultured and well read. They also formed social networks, getting to know each other in line, filling in for each other while they did other errands. The same thing happens in our country for teens camping out for twenty-four hours to get tickets to a concert, or for shoppers lining up overnight outside Macy's on Black Friday, or for sports fans queuing up for playoff tickets. In many cases, the wait becomes an adventure and more satisfying than its original purpose. It can even lead to a new romantic or business connection.

Hotels, restaurants, and other service providers have long understood that if a customer expects a certain level of service and perceives the service received to be higher than expected, he or she will be a satisfied customer. One of the trade secrets of crowded, trendy restaurants is to add an extra ten to fifteen minutes to the wait time they tell their customers. Then when a table becomes available earlier than anticipated, customers are pleased and start the meal impressed with the restaurant's efficient service and personal attention. Another key technique businesses use to relieve boredom arising from a sudden hole in time is to fill it up with something interactive. By placing mirrors in the waiting area by its elevators, one hotel found that it reduced complaints of long wait times: people love to look at themselves. And it's amusing to know that the "Close" buttons in elevators are usually mere placebos, intended to give people something to punch while they wait for the doors to shut. In doctors' and dentists' offices, the old standby of leafing through *National Geographic* and *People* is giving way to more dynamic pastimes such as gazing at large full-color anatomy charts and other visual or audio devices that allow patients to educate themselves about the human body.

At an individual level, there are also creative solutions. Take Christopher, a twenty-nine-year-old office worker who lives in suburban Boston. Commuting to work by car and paying for a parking garage became so expensive and time-consuming that he changed to public transportation. Now instead of sitting in gridlock twice a day, he enjoys the brisk fifteen-minute walk to the bus station. There is always something fresh and new to observe, and he is mastering the fine art of smiling at strangers. Lately, he has also taken up writing haiku, the pithy Zen-like poems that originated in Japan. Every day he strives to write at least one verse, distilling a poignant or memorable experience, thought, or feeling. And when he's stuck in line at the bank or barbershop, the experience is grist for his mill as he keenly observes what's happening around him. Traveling back and forth to work for Christopher used to be wasted time, or so it seemed to him. Now he's found a creative pursuit that makes him look forward to it.

Master the lost art of waiting, and you will make friends with time and grow less bored, irritated, or annoyed. Living in the eternal moment will exceed your greatest expectations. This is the exuberant Tao of Now, or Way of the Present.

Here are some further practical tips on waiting that will put you—not the clock—in charge:

1. PICK THE LONGEST LINE AT THE CHECKOUT COUNTER. That way, you won't be disappointed. And to your surprise, you may find that it moves more quickly than the lines around you. Smile at the frustrated customers (that used to be you!) who picked the shortest one. By just walking to the back of the longest line, you can transform the atmosphere in the room, slow down the pace, and change peoples' perception of time.

2. CHANT SILENTLY. Chant "*Om mani padme hum,*" the main Tibetan Buddhist mantra, or any other calm, peaceful chant, to soothe your mind and spirit and bring you back to center. Or memorize and recall your favorite poems.

3. DISCOVER THE SPACE AROUND YOU—the rhythm of the sounds, the texture of the setting, the voices and movement of those in your midst coming and going. Don't label. Simply relax into time and take it all in.

4. DO THE SHUNI MUDRA, HOLDING THE TIPS OF YOUR MIDDLE FINGER AND THUMB TOGETHER. This is a classic hand gesture or silent meditation for cultivating patience. These fingers are associated with the lung meridian and the heart governor meridian, respectively, and will harmonize your breathing, circulation, and Chi energy flow. This works anywhere, anytime: in line, arguing with your spouse, meeting with your boss, or jetting across the country.

Life is full of surprises and disappointments, delays and interruptions. The mere fact that we have to wait from time to time doesn't mean we have to put our mindfulness, good humor, and kindness on hold. While you're waiting for something else to happen, your life is still your life.

Cultivating Silence

Another way we can find time within time is by developing the right relationship to silence. For many people, silence can be uncomfortable. The small self feels naked and exposed, anxious, unproductive, or afraid of boredom. Noise is a way to cover up self-consciousness. We talk fast when we're nervous. We turn up the music so we won't bore our visitors if we run out of things to say.

Our world has become so filled with noise and other forms of sensory stimulation that there are fewer and fewer places to be found where we can withdraw, even for a few moments, and not hear some evidence of our high-tech world. Even mundane occupations, like taking out the trash, working out on exercise machines, or going for a walk are not always times when we can let our minds drift and be alone with our thoughts. Too often they become occasions to wire our heads up to hear music, news, podcasts, or audio books—or to carry on an electronic conversation.

When it comes to changing the pace of your busy life, the first step is to treat yourself to some silence. Take a breath; take a break. With silence and relaxed breathing, we automatically slow down.

I remember once in the mid-'70s when my parents came from their home on Long Island to visit me in Woodstock, New York. At the time I was helping to establish a Tibetan Buddhist monastery atop Meads Mountain and was living in a rented cottage out in the woods, where the original Woodstock utopian art colony had started earlier in the century. My suburban mother was worried about where to shop in the wilderness. How relieved she was to find that there was a supermarket in town, and a pharmacy chain, too, so that we wouldn't have to hunt and forage for our dinner.

After one night with only the sound of crickets, she fretted: "It's too quiet here; I'm afraid something's wrong—it's like a World War II blackout. How do you live up here?" She had spent her whole life in an urban or suburban environment and was deeply uneasy without any background din.

This is becoming more and more the case for all of us: even when we try to create silence, we have to practice tuning out some sort of artificial sound. How many people today habitually keep the TV or talk radio on all day just so they won't be lonely or have to deal with the absence of sound?

Think of what it's like when the power goes off. No more humming of the fridge, whirr of the hard drive, grind of the dishwasher, or sound of central heating or AC kicking in. Interestingly enough, on long meditation retreats—from one month to three months and more—people usually report that it was much harder ungluing themselves from their daily lives to get there than actually being there. As much as they might have feared the long hours and quiet, and missed their loved ones and favorite pastimes, they often say that they don't want to leave and return to the busyness, noise, and trivia of their regular lives.

As I've mentioned, Buddhists often practice Noble Silence in intensive meditation retreats, or Loving Silence. Even though we are in a group, we are alone with ourselves and our mindfulness practice and contemplations of impermanence, interconnectedness, loving-kindness, and selflessness. In the sharing circle we usually conduct at the end of weeklong retreats, new students often say they were initially most afraid of the idea of being silent for the entire time. But it usually turns out to have been the best part of the retreat for them, and a real relief, because they didn't have to socialize and worry about putting their best foot forward or pretending to be someone they're not. They found peace and serenity just being in their own skin, in the meditation room, in the dining room eating quietly, and in their room or the woods alone.

Of course, there is a Middle Way between becoming a Trappist monk who takes a lifelong vow of silence and listening to your MP3 player all day. You can begin to master your own pace. We spend so much of our days simply reacting. As we learned in "Reaching for Your Higher Self," the "Mindful Moments" section in chapter 2, you don't have to immediately answer your e-mails unless they are urgent. The world around you will not come crashing down, and you will actually have more time to focus on the big issues of your life. When you do respond to your e-mails, I recommend that you take a mindful pause before you hit "Send." Or try to observe a prayerful minute of silence before and after meals. This contemplative moment of intention will help ground you and stop the process of instinctually moving from one thing to the next without appreciation or awareness.

Earlier I mentioned the practice of waiting a few moments after the telephone or doorbell rings before responding, instead taking a moment to breathe and relax. Punctuating the day with these little moments of mindfulness can help break up the claustrophobia of feeling pressed for time by letting the cool, fresh air of nowness-awareness blow through. It will refresh and revive your spirit, awaken your energy, and enhance your feeling of both time and space. It is easy to spend large parts of our lives just reacting to the external stimuli around us. Taking opportunities to pause and reflect will help to keep you in the moment and become grounded in awareness and more attuned to your thoughts and feelings, values and priorities.

All Together Now

One of my longtime friends and colleagues is Stephan Rechtschaffen, M.D., one of the cofounders of the Omega Institute for Holistic Studies, a pioneer spiritual and health education center in Rhinebeck, New York. As a medical doctor, Stephan has long been interested in the effects of stress and has done his own thoughtful research on the pace of life, sharing his wisdom

in lectures and workshops as well as in *Timeshifting,* his book about alter-
ing our relationship to time. In it, he points to the phenomenon of *entrain-
ment* as one reason we can feel so rushed.

Since nothing happens in isolation, and our very DNA is programmed
to resonate with everything else in the universe, we are innate harmonizers.
Put two clocks (the old-fashioned kind, with pendulums) ticking away side
by side, and before long they will be ticktocking in unison. We're no different; because we're social creatures, when we walk down the street with
someone, we subconsciously try to move in sync with that person's gait.
When we converse, we synchronize gesture, posture, tone, and breath. Our
nervous systems naturally attune to those who are close to us; this capacity for empathy and nonverbal connection is known as *limbic resonance.*
Lovers and best friends often think the same thoughts and mirror each
other's moods, postures, and expressions. Parents and young children can
sometimes find themselves in amazing psychic harmony. Dogs, cats, birds,
and other pets also easily absorb our vibes and can after a while begin to
act, obsess, relax, and even look like us. Being out of rhythm with those
around us is discomfiting, and we unconsciously make tiny adjustments all
the time to rectify any mismatch.

If everyone around you is madly rushing around, competing for your
job, investing twice the hours in ensuring that their child will get into a great
college, battering you with e-mails, texting you and demanding an instant
reply, manicuring their home, yard, car, and body parts, it's pretty much a
given that you're going to unconsciously feel pressured and begin *entraining,*
or going along with, that hyperactive rhythm. Try strolling leisurely down a
crowded street in New York City during rush hour. It's not easy to resist going
with the flow—which is more like a torrent or flood than a gentle stream.

Sometimes you think you're managing just fine, so you ignore those
subtle signs that you're off-kilter—like not being able to shut your brain

down at night and sleep without a pill. If you're lucky, when your vacation comes around you fly off to some tropical island. After seven days, you have finally entrained to the gentle pace of life on the beach. You're sleeping nine or ten hours a night without any medicinal help, and your pace has slowed down drastically. Your preoccupations and work worries are for the most part gone and forgotten. *Why isn't life like this always?* you wonder. It could be! *What if I lived here? Would it be possible?* You come home refreshed and determined to take care of yourself. Your serene resolution lasts until you open your in-box to find five hundred messages or discover that the basement is flooded.

At such times, rather than immediately jumping back into the fray, the best approach is to make a date with yourself, sit down, and really look at what needs to be different. Don't allow yourself to simply go on automatic pilot. Vacations make you think about time differently. Now bring that practice into your daily life. In the next chapter I'll talk about the *sacred pause*. It's a way of saying, "I am." It is a way of saying, "Stop." It is a way of saying, "No," while saying, "Yes," to yourself. It's the first step in avoiding becoming a part of the herd and conforming to the frenetic short-term solutions, harmful ideologies and practices, and other social pressures around us. You'll create space in your pace when you learn instead to entrain to the rhythms of earth and sky, your own biological clocks, and people who walk their talk and set a bright, shining example.

TIME OUT

I Am I

This stress-reducing meditation can be done while sitting at your desk, while driving, while on a walk—just about anywhere—and can keep you from feeling overwhelmed by the pressures, deadlines, and

challenges of daily life. I have students who are professional performers who recite it as a mantra before going onstage. It centers
you fast and, after some practice, can be done in just a few seconds.

Remember/say/reflect to yourself (or aloud):

I am I; I am not I.

Repeat this affirmation again and again while taking slow, deep
belly breaths.

I have feelings, I am not my feelings.
I am I.

(Belly breath)

I have thoughts, I am not my thoughts.
I am I.

(Belly breath)

I have body sensations, I am not my body sensations.
I am I.

(Belly breath)

Then add your most current concern: stress, time, love, hurt, overwhelm, fear, anxiety.

I feel stressed, I am not my stress.
I am I.

(Belly breath)

I feel overwhelmed, I am not my overwhelm.
I am I.

(Belly breath)

I feel pressured with time, I am not my pressure with time.
I am I.

Substitute your emotions or anything that's upsetting you.

I feel hurt, I am not my hurt.
I am I.
I feel angry, I am not my anger.
I am I.

(Belly breath)

I am here, centered and free. Yes!
I feel jealous, I am not my jealousy.
I am I.

(Belly breath)

I have worry, I am not my worry.
I am I.

Or the body:

I have aches and pains, I am not my aches and pains.
I am I.

(Belly breath)

Now, while breathing, smiling, relaxing, letting go, and walking forth free and unencumbered, go fearlessly and boldly onstage into your life.

Visualizing Peace

My friend Bob is a building contractor who is always dealing with clients who want him to finish fast so they can reclaim their homes. He has a useful tool for calming himself down when he feels overwhelmed by time pressures and forces out of his control—like the weather, and subcontractors who don't always come through. He stops his truck and pulls over (or stops walking).

"I imagine I am gliding on my bicycle along a trail where we always vacation, in Maine. I picture myself inhaling the clear, clean air deep into my lungs, I feel the breeze on my face, I smell the ocean, and I hear the gulls squawking. This clears my head like a minivacation and brings me back to myself. Construction is how I make my living. It's not a matter of life and death that's worth getting in a frazzled state over."

Bob has the right idea. Another way to center yourself when time pressures threaten to stress you out is to tap into your own internal energy. Try this simple attention exercise, and you'll see what I mean.

1. Take a few slow, centering breaths.

2. Relax, and focus your mind on a point in the center of your hand.

3. Imagine that you are sending breath right into that point and that it is expanding and getting warm.

4. After a minute, compare the feeling in that hand with the other.

5. Rest at ease, and gently experience whatever it is, basking in the afterglow.

Most people who try this exercise feel some kind of sensation—heat, prickling, pulsing, or vitality—in the point where the mind was focused. The science of biofeedback is based precisely on the fact that people can use their minds to direct attention to specific areas of the body in order to lower blood pressure, slow heart rate, and decrease pain.

Of course, Tibetan meditators—monks, nuns, and yogis—have known about mind power for centuries and even millennia. Witness, for example, their practice of *tummo,* in which they cultivate the ability to raise their body heat so high that snow will melt in the area where they are sitting outdoors in lotus posture.

Once you have learned to center yourself in the midst of time pressures and stress, you can compassionately spread this feeling of relaxation outward, and benefit others by helping them get in sync with you. When you're speaking with a rushed or agitated friend or colleague, for example, take a deep breath, connect to your higher Self, and modulate your voice and breathing in an upbeat and calm way. This allows the other person to entrain to your more deliberate and skillful pace, and is beneficial and productive for both of you. Try it and see.

The Five Perfections

In the Diamond Path of Tibetan Buddhism, the Five Auspicious Perfections (or the Five Certainties) teach us to awaken the primordially enlightened heart-mind within us. This elegant, multileveled teaching purifies our perceptions and serves as an antidote to being closed, turned away, inattentive, distracted, jaded, or cynical. It opens us up to the infinite potential inherent in each moment. It frames our experience in a crystalline lattice in which time has five unique dimensions. It points to the absolute, timeless dimension that is simultaneously within and beyond us throughout our lives.

Cultivating these Five Perfections helps enhance our receptivity to and trust in the order of nature and our faith in our potential and ourselves. The Five Perfections empower the learning process on all levels, conscious and unconscious; facilitate the transmission of transcendent wisdom; and maximize the intended transformative results. The classic Five Perfections are the following:

1. Perfect Time.

This very moment is the *perfect moment.* This very time is the very first, fresh and pure, dreamlike instant, the highest heaven. This moment is the Golden Age, as during the lifetime of the Buddha, Jesus, Muhammad, or other great teachers, for they are still speaking to us today.

2. Perfect Place.

This place where we are is the perfect place. This very location is the *perfect space,* paradise, utopia, a radiant and stainless mandala or gathering of higher consciousness. Heaven is not just a place of bliss and endless delight that we go to after we die; it's right here and now. Just open your eyes and behold.

3. Perfect Teaching.

This is the timeless teaching, the ultimate, absolutely true and candid, direct, spontaneous enlightenment teaching, perfectly liberating and freeing. This perfection is not meant to be comparative; it simply asserts that *this* is the perfect teaching for here and now, for those who are listening and receiving it. This, what is, right now—not necessarily our particular doctrine or tradition, but the truth shining in this moment. Everything is sublime, as it is, in this very instant.

This moment's teaching, whatever you're getting, is the perfect teaching. If it's silence, this is the perfect teaching. If it's birdsong or traffic noise—that's it. If it's a harsh lesson or confusing, this, too, is it. None other to seek or long for; utmost reality is encoded in it, right here and now. The noble Dharma, or liberating Truth, is being eloquently expressed right here and now, for those with unobstructed ears to hear and eyes of pure vision to see. The sound of the stream is the song of the divine; the wind in the trees, the breath of the Goddess. Those around us are our *sangha,* the congregation or holy community of bodhisattvas and seekers.

4. Perfect Teacher.

The Absolute Buddha (or God, Allah, or Brahman) is the ultimate teacher, who is coming through here and now in various forms and guises. Its energy manifests itself through human (and, at times, avian, animal, and other nonhuman) teachers with their limitations and foibles, serving as vehicles for the underlying radiantly shining emanations—clear as a ringing bell that awakens you from a deep sleep.

5. Perfect Student.

This auspicious certainty is probably the hardest, the most challenging, for most of us to get. "What?" the inner defendant screams. "Who, me? I'm far from perfect." Yes, you can be the right channel for this truth. This fifth certainty is also termed "the perfect entourage," recasting the teacher–student relationship as the Buddha and his closest disciples (or the followers of Jesus, Muhammad, Gandhi, Gandalf, Yoda, or whomever you most respect).

Once, during a three-year meditation retreat deep in the forest in southwestern France, an American student said to our teacher, Dudjom Rinpoche, "Rinpoche, I get this; what could be better than this? This is obviously the perfect place. This is definitely the right place. This is the right moment. This is the right teaching, and you are the perfect teacher. But I don't feel like I'm the right person." How honest, how human, and how true! Even if we might have little questions with the first of the four perfect certainties, that fifth one is the really tough one for most of us. Why do we doubt ourselves to such an extent?

The Five Perfections point to the inner certainty leading directly from here to right here and now. Use this template to reframe your life, find genuine meaning and substance, and catapult yourself into a larger reality. It can completely transfigure your perception, understanding, and experience of time, space, and the meaning inherent in the moment.

It sanctifies each breath you take, each thought or feeling you experience, and each person you meet. The Five Perfections are a transformative teaching, hidden in plain sight in each moment. By skillfully changing the pace within our lives, we can enjoy a new spaciousness where they flower. This inner alchemy lays the groundwork for turning profane or ordinary time and space into the sacred. Remember the discussion of *drala* in chapter 1? Even though we persist in a habitual (di)vision of our world into two—the sacred and the profane—it's all really one perfect and complete world. When we can see it in the light of radiant awareness, we can transform it through the magical powers of awakened mind.

In the next chapter, you will learn to create or fashion temporal and special refuges—the foundation for putting forth your best efforts and realizing your life's full potential. You will learn how to entrain more effectively with others, renew yourself on retreats, and appreciate the transformative powers of music. Each new way of seeing brings you closer to living in Buddha Standard Time.

7

Living in Sacred Time and Space

Give thanks for unknown blessings
already on their way.

—Native American saying

EVERY SEVEN YEARS DESIGNER Stefan Sagmeister shuts down his New York business and takes a sabbatical—a year off for creative refreshment and personal renewal. A daring decision, he admits, but one that has led to increased productivity, more time to enjoy life, and a rich new crop of ideas after each period of rest.

Sabbatical, like the word *Sabbath,* comes from the Hebrew *Shabbat,* which means "rest" or "cessation." Shabbat is the seventh day of the Jewish week and a day of rest in Judaism. It recalls Genesis, the biblical account of how God created heaven and earth in six days and rested on the seventh. It also recalls the giving of the Torah at Mount Sinai, when God commanded the ancient Hebrews to observe the seventh day and keep it holy. Why is the number seven significant? The ancient Hebrews used to mark time by the twenty-eight-day lunar calendar, a template of actual celestial rhythms. The first day of any month was determined by the sighting of the new moon. Thus, when God in the Old Testament decreed a day of rest after six days of work, it was for one of the four times of renewal in a lunar cycle.

Today, as I discussed in chapter 1, most of us live in utter disregard for these natural cycles. We are typically unaware of the rising and setting of the sun, the waxing and waning of the moon, and the aspects of the planets. We enjoy or tolerate each shift of the seasons or weather—summer and winter, rain and snow, drought or wind—without much awareness of the dynamic forces of the earth and its voyage through the cosmos.

One of nature's greatest lessons concerns the cycle of constant renewal. In this chapter, we'll look at ways of renewing ourselves by recognizing or creating sacred time and sacred space. They are essential to transforming ourselves and the world in which we live, maintaining the energy and vitality we need to realize our goals on our life's journey, and awakening to a larger, timeless reality—a new vision of ourselves that accounts for our purpose in being here together in our interconnected world.

The Sacred Pause is the practice of creating a moment to respond more consciously—such as by breathing, attending, waiting, and considering things objectively—before reacting. Taking and making the Sacred Pause gives us more room to breathe, spiritually and mentally, refreshes us, and aligns us with how things are in the moment. In this heightened state of attention, we can respond more intelligently and intentionally.

I have a student named Melody who began to practice the Sacred Pause to deal with her tendency to procrastinate, which would paralyze her whenever she had to finish a report for her boss. She would obsess over details, feel overwhelmed by all the data she had collected, and get writer's block when it came to committing her thoughts to paper. "I could never meet my deadlines," Melody confessed, "and would invent all these excuses to give my boss for why I hadn't finished." When her internal anxiety and mental static became overwhelming, she came to me for guidance. When we talked about it, she realized that her blocks were caused by her relentless regrets and self-recriminations about the past ("Why didn't I get more done on this yesterday?") and anxieties about the future ("What if my boss doesn't like this?"). I encouraged her to focus on the present moment, our true home and natural refuge.

A few quiet breaks several times a day with the "Breathe, Smile, Relax" meditation enabled her to center and stay in the present. Her internal blockages started to lift, and now the imaginative energy that once impeded her progress is productively channeled into her work. We usually don't realize how much effort we put into avoidance and procrastination—effort that can be redirected toward achieving the very things we are putting off. "My boss was stunned when I turned my latest project in a day early," Melody recounted proudly. "He actually complimented my efficiency."

In order to feel truly balanced and nourished deep in our souls and put forward our best efforts, we need more than the kind of meaningful pauses and breaks that Melody learned to take; we need to access sacred time and sacred space. When we align our smaller, even cellular, self with nature's larger, outer macrocosm, we regain the feeling of truly being one with the Tao, or cosmic flow. Our small self returns to its true pace within the greater context of our higher Self. This practice cannot help but affect us to the core and give us the patience, courage, energy, and discipline not only to abide in the moment, recognize the connections, learn the lessons, realize goals, and help sustain others, but also to fulfill our human potential and achieve a state of transcendental unity and oneness.

Sacred and Profane Time

In *The Myth of the Eternal Return,* religious philosopher Mircea Eliade described how ancient cultures, and some strongly religious cultures today, recognize two kinds of time: sacred and profane. Sacred time is celebrated in religious festivals, whereas profane time is experienced in our ordinary, everyday life. In the ancient world, a culture's creation myths were reenacted in regular celebrations on such occasions as New Year's, the solstices or equinoxes, or other special days. Participating, for example, in the myth of how the cosmos was formed meant stepping out of ordinary time and into sacred time, and reliving the creation.

By the time of the Roman Empire, the most extreme rites in these festivals, including cannibalism and human sacrifice, had long been abandoned. In early modern times, sacred time continued to be observed during Carnival or Twelfth Night in Elizabethan England, when a Lord of Misrule was anointed as monarch for a day and everyone sang, feasted, flirted, and had a rollicking time. Today sacred time is still observed during Mardi Gras, the colorful pre-Lenten festival in New Orleans; Holi, the Hindu religious festival celebrating the end of winter, during which students daub their teachers with face paint, throw colored powders, and play pranks; and Eid at the end of Ramadan, the Islamic month of fasting.

Sacred time traditionally marked the rebirth of life, the return of order out of chaos, and a time of forgiveness and renewal. Ordinary time ceased during these observances, and the usual laws and customs of society remained suspended. Dances, mime, storytelling, and dramas reenacted the time of origins. Debts were often forgiven, prisoners released, differences reconciled, and other unfinished business resolved. All strata of society could start over, fresh and renewed, unburdened by the sins, injustices, or weight of the past. Time began anew.

Sacred time is cyclical rather than linear, because nature's rhythms are circular and spiraling. The Tibetan calendar I keep on my desk is crammed with notations about the best times throughout the year for remembering and honoring birth and death dates and beneficial activities of certain divine beings and historical figures, as well as for cultivating virtuous thoughts and performing altruistic acts. Instead of the twelve-month solar calendar of the West, Tibetans, like the ancient Hebrews and many other cultures today, continue to organize life according to the cycles of the moon.

When I lived in Asia during the '70s and '80s, almost every day some harvest festival, sun or moon cycle, equinox, solstice, or local tribal New Year was being observed with joyful celebration, prayers, chanting, fasting, and feeding the poor. Every month at full moon, my Tibetan teachers in Darjeeling, West Bengal, used to buy fish and birds, turtles, and other living creatures at the marketplace and release them back into the wild. They believed that a cosmic turning point, such as a full moon or eclipse, solstice or equinox, multiplied the effects of their compassionate deeds and brought extra merit—enhancing their good karma, and even extending their own health and longevity.

Although the practice of acting selflessly for the purpose of getting something back (extra karma points) might seem a little self-serving, there is no question that generosity is good for the soul. What you sow, you reap. Our good karma is vastly increased if we raise our gaze and open our hearts to include others in our prayers and aspirations. And if the stars and planets happen to be aligned auspiciously? All the better and more profoundly powerful. Why not accept a cosmic boost?

Sacred Synchrony

Chronos was the name of the Greek god of time. As we learned in chapter 3, the word *synchrony* means "together in time." When you are in synchrony with the sacred, you enter a different dimension of awareness where you can experience the essential teaching "as above, so below." From time immemorial, people have celebrated holy days and worshipped at holy places, such as stone circles, caves, the confluence of rivers, and churches, temples, and mosques. All of these places carry a certain energy and vibration, either from their unique natural materials, location, or design, or from the collective mind and spirit of the people who frequent them. They are imbued with energy, or Chi. When we visit holy places such as the Great Pyramid, the cathedral at Chartres, Stonehenge, old Jerusalem, Benares, or Lourdes, we immediately feel uplifted as the powerful natural energy or *drala* of the site or the accumulated prayer-energy of generations of faithful pilgrims recharges us.

Though we live in a secular society, most of us feel something special on New Year's, Christmas, Hanukkah, Halloween, Super Bowl Sunday, and/or other holi-/holy days. There is an energy and vibration that you pick up on, even if you aren't a believer or fan. For those who like to say it's only in your mind, I'd suggest delving more comprehensively into the challenging question of what isn't.

Besides the natural energies of the earth and our individual and collective consciousness, which imbue time and space with meaning or sacredness, there are celestial cycles that govern our destiny. These include the cycles of the constellations, the sun and planets, and the moon and asteroids, as well as the incoming waves and vibrations from our home galaxy, the Milky Way, as well as from the billions of galactic structures in deep space. All of these celestial bodies radiate subtle energies that shape and influence earthly events.

In Buddha Standard Time, every moment is potentially sacred, so it's really not necessary to go to church, temple, or Yankee Stadium, or to stop making any major decisions in your life, when, say, Mercury is in retrograde. We always have the potential to live fully in each moment and connect with the divine or timeless dimension. Yet, rediscovering traditional ceremonies and liturgy, participating in contemporary rituals, and studying astrology are all ways for many of us to get a glimpse of higher, deeper reality. Every home is a temple, and this earth is like an altar upon which we walk in the splendor of our renewed vision of expansive time and space.

In our postmodern age, we are far less interested in cosmology, rites, and rituals than in effective, science-based practices, tools, and effective techniques to help us fix our daily problems. Mindfulness-based stress reduction (MBSR), as developed and taught by Jon Kabat-Zinn, M.D., for example, is a timeless Buddhist-based contemplative technique to find a refuge in ordinary, everyday time. It has become part of the mainstream through hospitals and healing centers in the United States and abroad. It is also an excellent route into deeper spiritual practice and entering the now.

As effective as stress reduction can be, it's important to recognize that there is a difference between mere relaxation on the one hand and renewal conducive to spiritual development on the other. There are all sorts of activities that help you kick back, feel better, and be more productive. You can exercise, nap, luxuriate in bed with a good book, get a massage, take a walk, work on a favorite project, take a long, hot bath, make love—and after such experiences, there's no doubt you can go back into the fray with more resolve, determination, and peace of mind. But these restorative activities do not always result in deep renewal, long-lasting regeneration, and spiritual liberation. They are the equivalent of profane time, experienced by the small self. You enter sacred time when you step out of your ordinary state, embrace your higher Self/Buddha Mind, and intentionally raise your consciousness to a higher level. I'll show you how.

Renew Yourself on Retreat

According to explorers, there is a rare bird in the Amazon that stops singing between Friday evening and Saturday evening. On the other six days of the week it sings its heart out. You can learn a lot from this bird with its regular cycle of rest. Spending time at a retreat center is a powerful way to renew yourself in sacred time for a day, a weekend, a month, or longer. Places like Kripalu Center, in Western Massachussetts, and the Esalen Institute, in the Big Sur country of California, offer numerous work-exchange scholarships for retreats lasting from a single weekend to years. My own *Dzogchen* center offers over half a dozen residential meditation retreats each year. There are also various monasteries that open their doors to visitors seeking retreat.

In the Tibetan tradition, the unique three-year, three-month, and three-day contemplative monastic retreat training for lamas—which I twice completed—is a complete overhaul of body, soul, and spirit. When it is completed, the practitioner is transformed, renewed, and reborn all the way down to the cellular level.

In a less drastic refuge from profane time, the custom of making New Year's resolutions represents an opportunity for some diligent self-scrutiny—looking at relationships and family, health, career, hobbies, politics, intentions, and aspirations. But many people do find the time and the will to take a true retreat. Even Bill Gates, the enormously busy and productive philanthropist and founder of Microsoft, has his regular time of renewal, solitude, and silence. Gates spends at least one or two weeks each year at his rustic cabin in the mountains. There he lives by himself, reviews a stack of project proposals, and in solitude decides what new charitable or business ventures to pursue. Clearly, here is a stellar individual who recognizes that brief interludes, like Sabbaths and retreats, help regenerate the entire system. As we've learned in previous chapters, taking a break is not avoiding your life and responsibilities, but a skillful way to renew your focus and energy.

If you have extra energy and creativity on the full moon, sacred time for you might be spent in healing or prayer. If you become introspective and love to be outside and contemplate the splendors of nature as I do, when moonlight casts strange shadows across the land, you could conduct an all-night prayer vigil or take a solitary overnight hike.

Learn how to celebrate your birthday consciously, the anniversary of that time you appeared on the earth under a specific configuration of stars in the heavens. It is the perfect time for grateful appreciation of the gift of life and to reaffirm your genuine purpose for being here.

You can also take time out of the week, even a whole day, to simply *be.* Remember Marian Wright Edelman and her weekly day of silence? Consider putting such a day on your calendar and making it your own special festival of renewal, like your own personal Sabbath or contemplative retreat. I do this one morning every week, and turn myself over to spiritual reading, listening to music, meditation, and exercise. I try to get up by 6 A.M. on Sundays and stay alone and quiet—off the grid until at least noon. During my personal Sabbath I might go for a long walk, play the flute, sing, and even dance in the woods near my home, in addition to my usual meditations and chants, yoga, and praying. We might not attend a church or temple, but, like Emily Dickinson, we can find a cathedral in the trees sufficient, "and birds for preacher men."

Sacred Music and Sound

In Tibetan Buddhism we chant for several minutes before and after every meditation, and sometimes through the entire session. You might want to try it. There are wonderful Tibetan chants available on CD, and students report to me that in listening they find themselves transported to a timeless zone of serenity and solace. I find that any mellifluous music, such as Bach's Piano Nocturnes, is good for retreat and meditation. Sitar and flute music is wonderful, too. I like Erik Satie's piano pieces, particularly those on the CD *After the Rain,* performed by Pascal Rogé. For me, best of all are Mozart piano concertos, as well as piano music by Liszt, Chopin, and Rachmaninoff. Or put on some rocking dance music, reggae, or whatever makes you feel exhilarated, and have a solitary dance party. Feel the joy in being alive! This is your time to do whatever renews and refreshes you. And you can experiment with how the tempo of the music affects the rhythms and energy of your own body. Plato said, "Music gives a soul to the universe, wings to the mind, flight to the imagination, and life to everything." I like to joke that singing is believing.

Sound and music are a royal gateway to the sacred and timeless. The most exquisite music transcends all physicality, yet you may viscerally feel the vibrations of different sounds resonating in your body—in your solar plexus, for example—like a drumbeat. I remember hearing someone spontaneously compose and sing music of gratitude at the end of a weekend meditation retreat. He became like a flute himself—empty, straight, well tuned, and clear—as the mantric sound of *ahhhhhhi* emerged from within and around, embracing us all in the clear and transcendent space. I felt the sound resonating in my full body awareness, like ripples gently caressing a still pond. Music can transport us into the timeless, where we as observers merge and become one with the observed.

Curiously, human beings and songbirds are the only creatures that automatically move to the rhythm of a song. "The human heart wants to synchronize to music, the legs want to swing, metronomically, to a beat," explains Nina Kraus, a professor of neurobiology at Northwestern University who studies the effects of music on the nervous system.

Music and sound work their magic on us in several ways. The most basic is that music can slow down and equalize brain waves. As neuro-research shows, sound and music—including playing or listening to an instrument, singing, or other vocalizations—can modify brain waves. Music with a pulse of about sixty beats per minute can shift consciousness from the beta range to the alpha range. The beta range, as we saw earlier, represents ordinary waking consciousness, including negative emotions. The alpha state is characterized by heightened awareness, tranquillity, and more positive thoughts and feelings. Music in the sixty-beats-per-minute range includes certain Baroque, New Age, and ambient selections.

Music can also help us integrate the two sides of our brain. Playing Mozart, Bach, or other highly patterned classical music can stabilize our awareness, stimulate our mental focus, and increase our efficiency. It strengthens the logical, left side of our brain. Listening to Beethoven, Debussy, or other romantic, jazz, or New Age music, on the other hand, can enhance our intuition, creativity, and empathy and compassion for others. These genres strengthen the relational, right side of the brain.

In addition, music can alter our perception of time. When we are under pressure, orderly, left-brained music can help us make more efficient use of our time, and relaxing, right-brained sounds can reduce stress and tension. As a rule, bright, up-tempo music helps make time pass more quickly. Slow, heavy music slows it to a crawl.

Music also changes our perception of space. Slow music provides us more room in which to maneuver and relax. It can open up a confined space and enable us to feel lighter, freer, and more spacious. Conversely, fast music can help us set sonic boundaries and pathways within our environment, thereby increasing our drive and productivity.

In the East, mantras have long been recognized as a means to realization and fulfillment at many levels. A mantra is a sound, syllable, or phrase that can lead to physical, mental, and emotional or spiritual transformation. The most basic mantra is a single syllable like *ah,* which resonates in the lower intestines. The sound *m,* in contrast, vibrates much higher up in the body—in the throat or mouth. In between is the *u* or *o* sound that resonates in the central area of the heart and lungs. Repeating these sounds, out loud or silently, will stimulate these areas and strengthen their respective chakras, meridians, organs, and other structures and functions. When the three sounds are combined, they create the syllable *aum,* also spelled *om,* the most sacred mantra in Hinduism and Buddhism. Chanting a long, drawn-out *aum* stimulates all three regions, unifying mind, body, and spirit. *Aum* grounds us in the moment and has the potential to lift us beyond time and space. It symbolizes Primordial Vibration, from which everything springs. It can be recited to calm down and relax us or to put us in touch with our higher Self, to heal earthly ills or to elevate us to the music of the spheres.

In the West, chanting was once also a highly developed sacred art and science. Gregorian chant created the sonic structure for medieval and early modern Europe, telling the hours of the day and the seasons of the year. Its influence has echoed down the ages. In one French monastery in the 1960s, seventy of ninety monks suddenly became despondent and "slumped in their cells like wet dishrags." Doctors, psychologists, and nutritionists were summoned for their expert advice, but all remained stumped. Finally, the monastery's abbot turned to Alfred Tomatis, the pioneer medical doctor who first discovered that baby birds and humans in embryo could hear their parents' voices. Tomatis, known as "the Sherlock Holmes of sound and music," quickly diagnosed the malady. Following the relaxation of Vatican rules, several hours a day of Gregorian chant had been eliminated from the monks' daily routine. For years, they had been chanting together eight to ten times a day for ten to twenty minutes at a stretch. After the chanting was restored, the monks' breathing slowed down, their blood pressure normalized, and their mood and productivity went up. The magnificent *oooo*'s and sublime *eeee*'s in "Gloria in Excelsis Deo" and the repetitive pattern and alternating pitch of sustained Alleluias restored their joie de vivre.

In indigenous societies, songs and simple instruments were traditionally used to transport the listener into even deeper levels of consciousness. For example, shamanic drumming can take you into the theta range of brain activity, associated with deep sleep, hypnosis, out-of-body experiences, and other dimensions.

A Sound Retreat

This exercise is designed to transport you into *shicha,* the Fourth Time—the Tibetan Buddhist term for a transcendent dimension of timeless being that intersects each moment of horizontal linear time—past, present, and future. One of the most fascinating things about sound and music is that our responses to them are highly individualistic. What moves me may not move you, and what excites you may leave me cold. Whether it's a Mozart string quartet or a Buddy Holly classic, a *shakuhachi* flute or a rap riff, select something that resonates with you.

For beginners, I would recommend music without vocals or lyrics. For example, you could listen to the steady, emerging notes in Erik Satie's *Gymnopédie no. 1* as it moves you, step by step, note by note, into the very center of sound itself. Deep inside the core of the piece we find ourselves in Buddha Standard Time, stretching ourselves beyond the power of any ticking of the clock. The acclaimed violinist Joshua Bell carries us in the same way with each carefully drawn note of Saint-Saëns's *The Swan* or Massenet's *Élégie: O doux printemps d'autrefois.*

Experiment with the jazz sounds of John Coltrane on sax, and experience each note as it comes alive and springs from a place beyond abstract scores on a page or other conceptualization. Or check out impressionist Bill Evans's lovely piano compositions, focusing on note by individual note, one at a time, like beads on a rosary gently threaded together.

Or ring a gong, and follow—observing mindfully—the resonant note stretch out and fade, dissolving yourself at that event horizon. Then just rest gently in that spacious clarity and emptiness.

Further, with any of these selections, your own favorite, or the serenade of the birdsong outside your window early in the morning, get comfortable, let go of distractions, and allow yourself to simply rest and listen:

Breathe, smile, and relax several times.
Look deeply within and contemplate:
Who is hearing this music?
Where is it coming from? Where is it going?
Can you discern the silences between notes?
Rest in that openness, at home and at ease.

Listen to the Fourth Time—the timeless nowness. Stretch, expand, and dissolve deeply into time, and simply rest in the music.

Gradually, resume your ordinary awareness. Return to your everyday life renewed and refreshed from this brief voyage into sacred time and space.

Sacred Space

For over forty years, I have always kept a little altar or shrine of some sort, made out of furniture, logs, stones, cardboard boxes, crates covered with cloth, or whatever was handy and fitting. Such a space helps focus my meditation as well as my energies and daily home life. Now I have a meditation room in my home and I sit there first thing every morning for an hour, and sit there, however briefly, at night, too. Sometimes I keep a candle burning at the shrine all day, just to keep the practice space alive. Or I'll keep a night-light burning there day and night.

On the altar, I like to see a peaceful Buddha statue and some flowers or fruit offerings, incense, perhaps a crystal or special mirror to remind me of the timeless, ever-shining innate light of Spirit. Sometimes, during the day,

I just cruise by, wave, and say hi to my teacher's picture and the icons on the walls—just to cheer myself up. It's like putting myself through a little karmic drive-through car wash, and I come out brighter every time.

I also like to have a sitting Buddha stone statue in my garden that I can see from the kitchen or living-room window. Such an icon is like a mirror reflecting my higher Self.

If you think about sacred time as a dimension where we step out of our ordinary lives and our quotidian selves, this is also true for sacred space. Throughout the world, there are countless places that are sacred to the manifestations of a god or goddess, or to some miracle connected with sacred time. My understanding of a truly sacred place is one in which the interior feels larger than the exterior. In our homes today we have rooms set aside for physical workouts, television and games, music, computer workstations, and other mundane activities, but rarely do we find a room dedicated exclusively to self-renewal in the timeless dimension. Imagine the possibilities:

• A tree-house shrine or chapel

• A small shelf with sacred objects

• A closet, painted a glorious color inside, with shelves where special treasures from nature, as well as inspiring books and images, can be arranged. Take the door off, or close it to "maintain the energy" if you use the room for other activities.

• A room for yoga, meditation, prayer, and family circles

• A child's playhouse, renovated into a small chapel or temple

• A portable altar for your desk at work

• A music room or poetry room

• A sacred roof garden

It's amazing how a little adjustment to your ordinary, everyday space can affect your entire mood. Teresa, one of my students, had been meditating for many years. In the course of her practice, she had used many Buddhist *zabutons,* or cushions, to sit on. She installed tatami, the traditional thick straw Japanese mats, in her apartment. For a while she also used a small wooden seat made of maple that she could tuck her legs under in the Far Eastern *seiza,* or kneeling position.

Recently her friend Nadia, knowing her interest in spiritual development, gave Teresa an Islamic prayer mat for her birthday. It was inlaid with thin strips of agarwood from India and gave off a fragrant, musky aroma.

"It is extremely centering," Teresa told me after using it for a few weeks. "It simultaneously grounded me, rooting me to the earth, and uplifted my mind and spirit with its heavenly scent. The mat has significantly improved my practice." Though as a rule Muslims use a simpler, more basic prayer mat for their five-times-daily prayers than the elegant one Nadia gave her, Teresa learned what a powerful impact this accessory can have on one's consciousness. "It creates a sacred space around my entire being," she said. "Now I take it with me everywhere I go, and it immediately transforms the space." I myself have such a magic carpet, which I bought in Tehran in 1971.

Going on a pilgrimage is another way to cultivate sacred time and space. Doing so re-creates the spiritual journey into cyclical or timeless time and can be an annual practice, a onetime culmination of a life dream, a visit to a place of miracles for healing, or a mission to raise awareness about an issue, such as world peace, the environment, AIDS, or poverty. I still make pilgrimages to see my teachers, visit my home monastery in Nepal, and go to other holy sites, including the Wailing Wall in Jerusalem, sacred to my clan ancestors, and the Bodhi Tree in Bodh Gaya, India, under which Prince Siddhartha found spiritual enlightenment.

There are many such modern-day spiritual sojourners. I read about William and Alexandra Riggins, who set out on bicycles in 1998 to begin a pilgrimage to bring music and loving-kindness to wherever they found a calling to service. Thirty-seven thousand miles later, after countless visits to hospitals, senior centers, churches, orphanages, and retreat centers, they are still on the road, having bicycled all over Europe, Canada, and the United States. What began as a longing for renewal has become a way of life. Despite their lack of cash, they report that their needs are always met, since people along the way generously offer them food, shelter, and hospitality.

Every twelve years, when Jupiter moves into the zodiac sign of Aquarius (or *Kumbha,* a Sanskrit word for "water pitcher"), the greatest congregation of people in the world takes place in Allahabad, in northern India. This city is the site of the *sangham,* or sacred confluence, where the Ganges, the Yamuna, and the mythical underground Sarasvati Rivers join, and where it is said that the gods spilled a drop of the elixir of immortality. At what is renowned as the Kumbha Mela—the world's largest festival—millions of Hindus come together to perform ritual ablutions and other sacred prayers, chants, teachings, and discussions for days and even weeks on end. In 2001, as many as *60 million* made the pilgrimage. Imagine how highly charged this site must be from the confluence of three powerful rivers, a sacred mythical narrative, and the past, present, and future energy, vibration, and consciousness of hundreds of millions of pilgrims! Like Mecca, the focal point for billions of prayers every day, it is one of the most energized—holiest—places on the planet.

Any kind of pilgrimage can be one of the very best ways of "supercharging" our daily life. A prolonged time away from home is also a trip away from old habits and a well-worn comfort zone, and it can refresh our inner life. Sometimes we can experience new awakenings in such places, or access feelings we'd forgotten—perhaps since childhood. Such moments of grace remind us that the intellect can go only so far, and that perhaps our present life path is not entirely the one we need and long for. Or we can see our life anew, and discover—much to our surprise—that we already have everything we want and need.

The Tao of Travel

Whenever I am on a pilgrimage, a speaking engagement, or a vacation, I try to find a sacred space or inspiring place to go to daily. In Boston, it's the Buddha Hall inside the Museum of Fine Arts, with its enormous original statues brought from Japan long ago and set in a dedicated temple of their own. In San Francisco, it's the Japanese Tea Garden in Golden Gate Park, or atop Mt. Tamalpais at the ranger station, with its unparalleled view all over the outspread Bay Area. In Paris, it's towering Notre Dame Cathedral and the majestic bridges across the Seine.

But remember, it's the journey that's sacred, not the destination. Just traveling to a new place, a new country, or a new culture can be enlightening and remind us that time is elastic, not fixed. Zerina, a Scandinavian physician who volunteers her services to Third World countries whenever she gets a chance, recently returned from a visit to Mali, in West Africa. "My journey lasted twenty days, but I experienced it as three months," she recalls. "Every day was so full of encounters with people who lived, spoke, and valued things so fundamentally different from myself that it forced me to reflect and ask, What is really important to live a happy life?" Zerina says that part of her passion for travel and discovery of new places lies in "bringing me back to the present moment. I have to be there fully in order to capture what is going on." She says she feels like a child again, opening up the senses, seeing things for the first time. "I cannot rely on my habits, the autopilot is turned off, and I am fully awake." Present-moment awareness, embracing the senses vividly, enlivened her and enriched every one of her experiences.

Zerina, whose travels have included trips to Tibet among many other exotic destinations, quotes Marcel Proust: "'The only real voyage of discovery consists not in seeking new landscapes, but in having fresh eyes.' By being aware of opening our eyes, our minds, our hearts in our daily lives, we can start to experience people and situations from new and enriching angles, and what was true yesterday is not necessarily true today."

In her native Copenhagen, Zerina also has learned to live in the now. "Another way to come back to the present moment and have a feeling of eternity in front of you is by finding out what is important for you," she explains. "How do you want to live your life? What is most important? Spending time with people you love and doing things you love, or chasing after things that will give you temporary pleasure, prestige, or fame? My experience is that when I do things that I love to do, whether cooking, laughing with friends, walking in the forest, writing a poem in my favorite café, or helping my patients in the hospital, it brings me back to the present moment. Time somehow expands, and I feel I have all the time in the world."

We don't need to make a pilgrimage to Tibet, Mali, or the Boston Museum of Fine Arts to find a holy spot. Any nook or cranny will do: under a tree in the park or on a bench in the sun, in the basement or attic, on a rooftop or fire escape. Small portable altars can be set up anywhere. Or an altar can be created on the spot: nature willingly provides beautiful rocks, leaves, feathers, shells, driftwood, and even birdsong for the celestial choir and symphony of sacred time. You can also close your eyes and turn the spotlight inward, independent of external circumstances and conditions, and rest inside the still center of your own heart, as mystics and sages have done throughout the ages.

Perhaps you live in a noisy apartment with several kids and demanding pets. Include them in sacred time. Animals always catch the energy when it changes and settle down happily. Children treasure such memories of sacred time and follow your lead when they grow up. Maybe you don't have the luxury of extra space for a dedicated meditation, yoga, or prayer room. Think creatively; claim your sacred space. Invest yourself and get your Self back in return.

Ultimately, make sacred space wherever you are and sacred time each and every moment. Even when you feel far from the sacred zone, remember that it is never far from you.

Breaking Out of the Comfort Zone

At one point or another, everyone hits a plateau on his or her soul's journey, just as we do in other parts of our lives, whether it's our love life, dieting, learning an instrument, professional career development, or training for a marathon. This is why the practice of renewal is essential. The preeminent German author Goethe wrote, "We must always change, renew, rejuvenate ourselves; otherwise we harden." When creativity and vitality ebb, we need to break the pattern, just as sometimes we have to turn over a garden—uproot the old and start a new crop for the next season, or even let it lie fallow for a year or two to give the field time to regenerate.

My friend Kevin, a cancer survivor, sees things very differently since the illness hit. "I do not want to waste my time," he explains. "I'm watching my kids grow up today, and that's a miracle. This is grace, a gift I no longer take for granted in the rush of events, the waterfall of minutes and moments that so easily obscures my vision. I am a lot more conscious, and therefore discerning of my time and how I choose to be with it."

Sickness, hardship, and deprivation bring us down to essences. As we have seen with the story of Jill Bolte Taylor's illness, physical hardship can actually present an opportunity for beneficial life changes. A change in routine, a stretch of tired spiritual muscles, can help remind us that we are much more than we believe ourselves to be. Fasting for one day or longer, or holding a candlelight vigil, or going on a retreat or pilgrimage or sabbatical are all potent ways to change the habitual pattern of a life, discover the inner wellspring of ever-fresh natural resources within ourselves, and use our time more creatively and wisely.

Siddhartha left his sumptuous life in his father's palace and journeyed out into the world, seeking ways to pare himself down to his essence, and spent six years meditating, fasting, and practicing yoga in the wilderness until he attained enlightenment. Jesus spent forty days and nights in the desert, praying for illumination. Native Americans go on extended vision quests in the deserts and high mountains, endure the intense heat of sweat lodges, or pierce their flesh, fast, pray, go without water, and dance in the broiling sun for several days during their Sun Dance festivals in order to stretch beyond their habitual limits.

Fasting, renunciation, self-denial, and rigorous austerities have long been ways for humans to break out of the comfort of their daily existence—and especially out of ruts, stuck places, and old habits—in order to do a clean-out of the old and ring in the new. In denying our cravings and old habits, we can recondition and decondition familiar ruts and patterns. Try the following to accomplish this goal for yourself.

MINDFUL MOMENTS

Breaking Old Patterns

Here are some ways that you can break old patterns and experience the kind of renewal that will lead to better use of your time and energy:

- Go without speaking for a morning or a whole day.
- Skip a meal, or do an all-day fast.
- Take a break from technology—cell phones, computer, television, iTunes, you name it—for a prescribed period of time. (Base the time frame on a realistic goal.)

- Go on a news fast for a day, a weekend, or a week.

- Don't read anything at all for a day, a weekend, or a week; sit still, refrain from consuming the ideas and musings of other people, and be with your own thoughts for a change.

- For a prescribed period of time, don't talk about anyone who is not present, and notice how different this feels from the usual round of gossip and unconscious chitchat.

- Wake up an hour or half an hour earlier than usual, and use that time regularly for a trip into sacred time.

- Do an all-night vigil outdoors, next to a bonfire, on a mountaintop, or beside a body of water.

- Get off the energy grid for a day. Turn off the power in your house, and reconnect to a different kind of energy.

Right Napping

Closer to home or office, the virtues of the old-fashioned nap or siesta have been rediscovered by modern science. Far from taking time out of a busy day, a brief amount of shut-eye in the early afternoon relaxes, renews, and restores you so that you are much more productive and engaged during the rest of the workday. Power-napping is the newest oldest great thing, with Fortune 500 companies, sports teams, and other heavy hitters encouraging their executives and staff to take a nap in the early afternoon. "Rest is sacred," as the ancient scriptures of India say.

Many individuals have also found that the nap is not just for toddlers. In her blog, my friend Amy Hertz, editor of HuffPost Books, recently wrote about her lifelong struggle to sleep or stay rested. In an article entitled "Want to Be Smarter Than a Fifth Grader? Be a Better Napper Than a 2-Year-Old," she recounts how she stopped napping at age one. "I wore out my mother, father, and extended family during the day," she explains. "They tried bribing me and scaring me [into napping]. Nothing worked, and I lost the ability to nap."

Over the years, Amy's sleeplessness and restlessness only worsened. Ultimately, she came down with chronic fatigue syndrome and ended up "too tired to do anything but stare at the ceiling" and watch time pass her by. She turned for help to Western medicine, Chinese medicine, and then energy healing, but nothing worked.

Finally, she consulted Gelek Rinpoche, a venerable Tibetan lama in Ann Arbor, Michigan. "What do I do? What meditation practices? What retreats? Where do I go? I'll do any practice, just tell me," she implored.

"Every day, three times a day, lie down, close your eyes, and for ten minutes do nothing," the Buddhist master advised.

"Nothing? Can I listen to teachings?" she said.

"No, nothing."

"Can I write down ideas?"

"No, nothing. Just lie there and do nothing. Set an alarm if you have to."

So Amy took Rinpoche's advice. It took her a solid year of practice, but now, she says, "I can nap at will—almost anywhere—and even time myself without setting an alarm." She calls it the Nap Transmission. Here are the steps to take:

1. NO NEED TO LIE DOWN. Just close your eyes and unplug for several minutes.

2. LET YOUR MIND SETTLE AT THE HEART LEVEL, and begin to lightly notice the air from your breath passing through the region of your lungs and your Heart chakra.

3. DON'T GET UP UNDER ANY CIRCUMSTANCES. Don't write anything down. Don't look at the clock, but set an alarm if you like.

4. IF YOU'VE NEVER NAPPED, BEGIN WITH TEN MINUTES THREE TIMES A DAY. Eventually transition toward one twenty-minute nap daily.

Amy says she couldn't believe how much better she felt at the end of every day and how much more time and energy she now had, which utterly transformed her life. Try it for yourself, and discover how much better use you can make of your day.

I remember when the Dalai Lama was at our retreat center in southern France in the early '90s. It was hard to keep up with the pace of his constant service and attentiveness to the needs of others: his demanding schedule and 3:30 A.M. rising time, his nonstop grueling meetings, his travels without a break even in the evenings and on weekends. One day I said, "Your Holiness, can I stop now? I can't go on much more." He said, "Sure, you can. But just remember that you can't really stop until I do." He was talking about time and our universal, timeless mission and vow to help deliver all sentient beings beyond suffering and confusion and to nirvana-like peace, felicity, and bliss.

Everything we seek and long for—including joy, holiness, divinity, inner peace, and happiness—can be enjoyed in every moment, anytime, anywhere. The approaches and techniques to expand sacred time and space that we have looked at in this chapter—going on retreat, making a pilgrimage, celebrating holy days and holidays, taking a personal Sabbath, traveling, and napping—are simply vehicles to a state of timeless being.

In the next chapter we will take the view from afar, looking at a fascinating cosmic overview of historical time on earth. You will learn to experience sickness, loss, and other ravages of time with graceful acceptance. Here also is the place to speak of death and dying—and the movies.

CHAPTER

The Spinning Wheel of Time

The moment has no time.

—Leonardo da Vinci

WHEN WE ARE YOUNG, the passage of time can be a slow and sometimes frustrating experience. I remember endlessly waiting for the class bell to ring and let me out, or for the weekends, the winter holidays, and the long-awaited summer vacation that seemed never to come.

Time has always captured my imagination. At twelve, I used to skate on the frozen lake behind our suburban high school on Long Island, play ice hockey with my friends, speed and whirl around until dusk fell and our parents came looking for us, skidding across the frozen lake in their street shoes and suits. I loved to watch the streams of water and bubbles course beneath the ice, and, harboring a contemplative streak even then, I used to think, "Is this what time is like, flowing beneath my feet? Here I stand, stock-still, while the earth spins around and time runs on, yet gravity holds me down and makes everything feel solid, safe, and secure. How bizarre!

Where did all this come from? Who made it and keeps it ticking? What would time mean if the earth stood still, or didn't exist at all? What keeps everything from flying off into space?"

Gravity seemed a poor excuse for an explanation. Sometimes I wondered if my siblings and I were part of a strange experiment the adults had concocted to see how much we could be made to believe without rebelling against the implausibility of it all.

Many years later, on a wintry day near our Tibetan monastery atop Meads Mountain, in the Catskill Mountains of upstate New York, I remember watching in awe as the water cascaded beneath the frozen face of a waterfall. I suddenly recalled that twelve-year-old ice-skating suburban boy's reflections on the nature of time and life slipping past us, mostly without our notice. In that moment, as a thirty-year-old who was on the path of inner peace, I thought to myself, "Time is flowing in and through me, and I don't have to try mightily to get into the current. I don't need to get caught in a web of disturbing thoughts about its limitations on my life. It flows through me always, regardless of my activities, plans, or subjective interpretations and personal mythmaking. All this is as part of me as I'm a part of it. It is all in my mind. My mind is all of it."

Aging: "Going All the Way into It"

Today children are spending less time outside and in nature than I did as a boy, and I wonder about the time they have for contemplative pursuits. They also seem in many ways to be maturing faster than ever, with a whole new set of temporal demands. I was surprised to read in *Time* magazine a case against summer vacations for kids, since the downtime has been proven to interfere with their academic achievement in our highly competitive society. Children deal with mounting school pressures, and paying back student loans can mortgage their future well into adulthood. According to the U.S.

Department of Labor, it now costs a family $250,000 to bring up each child. Generating enough income, holding on to a job in a devastating economy, and balancing work and home life are daunting challenges for many parents.

The new cycles of youth, middle age, and aging have been in place for a while now, but for the most part we don't have corresponding rites of passage to help us appropriately prepare for and cope with the challenges on our time that each represents.

In middle age or maturity, we traditionally reach the peak fulfillment in our lives as we master (as well as we're probably ever going to) love, relationships, work skills, parenting, and other essential components of most lives. We experience time more deeply, more richly, and in a less adversarial way than when we were young. In the Chinese doctrine of the five stages of transformation, this period of life corresponds to balance. Everything reaches a stage of perfect harmony and contentment.

Of course, modern lifestyles rarely synchronize with natural time, so in middle age we can be as starved for time as at any other stage of life. In our particular era, unemployment, underemployment, stagnant wages and interest rates, and other economic woes mean that for many, instead of enjoying the time of their lives, they are living on meager incomes, watching as their homes are foreclosed upon, or scrambling to find work and overcome feelings of meaninglessness.

Old age has also undergone a dramatic change. In traditional societies, elders are venerated for their wisdom and actively sought out for their guidance. In the West, aging has long been a time of boredom, isolation, loss of purpose and relevance, and often deep loneliness as we sequester seniors in institutions to live out their days blankly staring at a television. In recent years, however, some assisted-living and nursing homes have transformed into a kind of resort hotel, where older people keep up an active life of travel, entertainment, dating and sex, and even new careers. I recently read about eighty- and ninety-somethings pushing the envelope—not the one from Social Security, but the challenge to scale Everest and accomplish other feats. The article featured pictures of an eighty-nine-year-old who made it to the North and South Poles and another of similar age who took up wing-walking, strapping his feet to the top of a single-engine biplane and flying across the English Channel at 160 miles per hour. Elder globetrotting has become one of the hottest segments of the international travel industry.

It's great to recognize that "you're only as old as you think you are." But at the same time, there seems to be no place in our culture where elders can give themselves to a higher purpose that includes passing wisdom on to younger generations, who too often grow up with digital avatars and media mentors rather than human ones. Where have all the wise men and women gone? In my youth, there were Albert Einstein, Albert Schweitzer, Bertrand Russell, Georgia O'Keeffe, Eleanor Roosevelt, Pablo Casals, Dr. Spock, and many others to look up to. Today, the only internationally renowned elders that come to mind quickly are Nelson Mandela and the Dalai Lama.

Our youth-oriented culture tends to see aging as a time of disempowerment and uselessness. How different it would be if the idea of slowing down and turning inward became an honored practice among the elderly. In the four stages of life recognized in Hinduism, the final years are designated specifically for that purpose. No more rushing. No more trying to make eighty into the new sixty. Stillness. Serenity. A time honored for cultivating perspective, deeper wisdom, vision and self-knowledge, understanding, empathy, and compassion.

My wise elder friend Rabbi Zalman Schachter-Shalomi has long advocated the concept of *spiritual eldering* as a viable process by which we can transform the downward arc of loneliness and isolation of the later years into a time of expanded consciousness. It could crown and ennoble a life. Reb Zalman calls it "aging and saging." Sounds much better than aging and disengaging.

A few years ago I was in Hawaii, on the island of Maui, for a retreat and had the good fortune to hear the aging slack-key guitar master George Kahumoku Jr. play, sing, and tell stories from his book *A Hawaiian Life*. (Slack key is a certain fingering style of guitar playing that originated in Hawaii.) He told one marvelous tale about his late aunt, who had taught him a unique slack-key style when he was a young boy. "She always played the same song over and over," he said. "Later, when I was a teenager and had lots of tunes in my repertoire, I was bold enough to ask her: 'Auntie, why don't you play something different? You know so many tunes; why keep playing the same thing?' She answered: 'You are young, you like new things and many different ones. That's fine. I am old now. Our old Hawaiian tradition is to like one thing a lot, and go all the way into it.'"

This is the wisdom of Elder Mind, the timeless Tao that cannot be named, recognizing that aging is a time of deepening and refining our wisdom. It is a time to nurture what should be passed on. It could also be the best years of your life. An apple can swell into a green orb on a tree for a whole summer. But in the fall, when the year is drawing into itself and wearing down into its wintry age—that is when the fruit ripens. As the traditional riddle puts it: when is the perfect time to harvest an apple? Answer: the moment it falls from the tree. So instead of thinking of old age as a time of withering, think of the kind of fruit your life could bear when you mature to ripe old age.

Suffering and Loss

It is true that time heals all ills, and the long view is worth keeping in mind. Yet wise sayings and clichés are of little comfort when loss and grief overwhelm us, when time appears never ending and we are in the midst of pain, misery, and fear that tear at the fabric of our souls. The only way to overcome it is to go deeper, looking closely at the suffering, gaining insight, and then moving through it onto the far shore of clarity and freedom.

Our wisest contemporaries deal with loss in different ways. Marion Woodman, a sage elder, Jungian analyst, and distinguished author, says when suffering grievously she feels and experiences the red blood flowing through her body. "Trusting that physical embodiment, I lean into the darkness of the experience to try to discover whatever gift it may have to give me," she explains. This is a good example of Full Connection Meditation.

Karla McLaren, author of *Emotional Genius*, takes another, more amusing tack. She employs a powerful healing practice she calls *conscious complaining*. She finds a quiet place and faces a wall, window, or altar. Or she goes outside into the yard and stands in front of a tree. Then she unleashes all her fury, complaining until she runs dry. When she's done, she offers a prayerful hand gesture, or mudra, and then goes off and enjoys herself. She vows that it works like a charm.

Peter Levine, the author of *Healing Trauma*, takes a more inward approach. He looks for that place in his body where he feels strongest and most vital. After focusing on that area, he moves on in a meditative scan to other areas, seeking to find where he experiences challenge or difficulty. "I don't try to fix it or even to understand it, but to feel it and experience it in my body, in my experience," he relates. "Then without judgment, as best I can, I shift my attention between the places I feel the strongest and those where I feel the distress." He goes back and forth between the stronger and weaker areas until a rhythm starts to emerge. Following that rhythm, he finds a new direction, and the path opens ahead.

In my own life I have found that it is only through acceptance and appreciation of our difficulties that we become fully developed human beings; often something must be relinquished in order for new growth to take place. Spiritual rebirth requires some form of loss or death. There is no other way to the light than through the darkness. It is a profound journey, and with each step of it we discover that the frightening shadows are nothing but various shades of the light.

One person emerges from a holocaust like a phoenix arisen from the ashes—Nobel Peace laureate Elie Wiesel, for example, who survived the horrors of Auschwitz as a child—while another emerges embittered, disillusioned, and ruined for life. Why do some people cling to the past and others let go? The reasons are complicated, but I do feel that very different outcomes from similar tragedies have to do with an individual's choices, understanding, faith, and hope, as well as other inner resources.

After particularly traumatic experiences, some people are prone to lose touch with the present when it becomes painful. What was once a life-saving and adaptive tendency—dissociating during periods of acute stress when young—can become habitual, unproductive, and self-destructive. In extreme examples, trauma survivors can frequently lose time—minutes, hours, or even days—in what is known as a *fugue state*. But I have found that once they learn to focus their attention on the now in order to reconnect and heal, they discover that they have immense capacities for spiritual growth, awareness, and healthy transcendence. In a way, we can look at the suffering in our lives as either *destructive* or *creative*—and we have the potential to transform ourselves either way.

God is found not only on mountaintops, but amid the ashes, too. This beautiful prayer was found in 1945 beside the body of a Jewish child in the Ravensbrück concentration camp, were ninety-two thousand women and children died:

O Lord,
remember not only the men and women of goodwill,
but also those of ill will.
But do not only remember the suffering they have inflicted on us,
remember the fruits we bore thanks to this suffering,
our comradeship, our loyalty, our humility,
the courage, the generosity,

the greatness of heart which has grown out of all this.
And when they come to judgment
let all the fruits which we have borne
be their forgiveness. Amen.

What can we do when our own grief threatens to overwhelm us, when the death of someone we love, serious illness, heartbreaking failure, or any crushing disappointment befalls us? Through my own practice, as well as years of teaching meditation, I have outlined some steps that can help guide us through change and loss and keep us from being crippled by them:

1. FACE THE LOSS. Be aware rather than in denial. Do not avoid the pain, fear, anger, anxiety, regret, anguish, despondency, or whatever other emotions you feel. Remember: awareness is curative. Let the light in, and you will find your way.

2. GO THROUGH THE HEALTHY, NECESSARY STAGES OF GRIEVING. These usually include some permutation of the following: (1) shock, denial; (2) pain, anguish, anger; (3) bargaining, negotiating; (4) sadness, despair, hopelessness; and (5) gradual letting go and eventual acceptance. Remember: your path is unique; in whatever order or form it occurs, there is an authenticity and emotional validity to your own natural process and pace of suffering and acceptance. Give it time. Don't rush the grieving process. But don't prolong it unnecessarily either. Find a Middle Way.

3. REMEMBER THAT THIS TOO SHALL PASS. Understand the impermanent, tenuous, dreamlike nature of things, and recite the Buddhist mantra: this too shall pass.

4. LEARN THE LESSONS. Recognize how things come about (cause and effect, or karma), and learn to steer a clearer course in the future

Examine your own beliefs and assumptions about the painful situation, its meaning for you, and its past and future implications. Remember: the guiding principle is to start wherever you are, with awareness and patience, and then to seek understanding.

5. PRACTICE PATIENT FORBEARANCE. One of the Buddhist principles on the Eightfold Path to Enlightenment is to develop inner strength, fortitude, resilience, tolerance, and the long-term view.

6. BREATHE IN AND OUT. Feel the pain, come to know it through examination and equanimity, and then release it. Remember: awareness is the key. Stay attentive, conscious, and intentionally awake—no sleep-walking through the difficult aspects of life.

7. EMPATHY AND COMPASSION. Let the experience of pain and suffering leave you feeling tender, vulnerable, and sensitive. Notice that others, too, are going through similar anguish, just as you have, and express empathy and compassionate kinship with them and their suffering. Remember: *brokenheartedness* can become openheartedness. Suffering is the greatest precipitate for spiritual change, inner growth, and transformation, and everyone experiences it at one time or another.

Death and Dying

The idea that we will one day cease to exist drives many people forward like a taskmaster who never puts down the whip. Woody Allen has a different take: "I don't want to achieve immortality through my work. I want to achieve it through not dying."

To Buddhists, the prospect of death is not something to be feared. On the contrary, the contemplation of our own mortality provides an opportunity and impetus for awakening—a gift that brings home both the imperma-nence and the preciousness and miraculous gift of life here and now.

How long is a life well lived? How can we celebrate the richness of the elder mind, age gracefully and intelligently, and contemplate our respon-sibility across the span of time to future generations and in the greater scheme of cosmic time and space? How can we pass on the best of what we have and who we are? What shall our legacy be?

The Tibetan Book of the Dead—a guide to the experiences that con-sciousness undergoes between death and the rebirth—counsels us to let go of our attachments as our time on earth draws to an end, and in the moment of death to focus on the Clear Light. Death and dying are a time to put our life into perspective, rejoice in the moments we had on this beauti-ful planet, resolve to do better in any future lives, and return gratefully to our source.

It takes a supreme degree of consciousness to transform dying into a spiritual practice and to awaken in the clear light as our physical elements dissolve and we pass on. One of the great goals of meditative traditions and the spiritual life is just this: to participate consciously in the unfolding of our lives, experiencing each stage fully, and remain aware through the pro-cess of, and even beyond, death. With a lifetime of paying mindful attention and cultivating focused awareness, even our own ends can be contemplated and experienced in sacred time, awakefully, with calm compassion.

Minding the Gap

In chapter 5, I introduced the concept of *bardo,* the Tibetan word for the in-between space. It can be short—a moment between thoughts or breaths or a momentary transition, such as Clark Kent changing into his Superman duds in a phone booth—or long, such as the passage toward becoming a teenager, an adult, or a senior. Am I an adult when I get a driver's license?

First have sex? Land a full-time job? Am I a senior at fifty-five, sixty, sixty-five? It takes a lot of self-awareness to be in the middle of uncertainty and still keep our wits about us. Just ask any adolescent caught between childhood and young adulthood.

There are also small, regular intervals in daily life that we often overlook. In every *bardo* in life, we need to learn to stay in balance with the flow and energy of what is happening around us. A good dancer feels the music and gives just the right amount of energy to stay in the flow. A good storyteller or comedian is said to have great timing because he or she knows the power of the pause before the punch line. Musicians know that the beat and the silence between notes are as important to the music as the notes themselves. Perfect timing is essential in all sports; the superb athlete must be acutely aware in that split second between cause and effect.

The best way to deal with the suspense of a *bardo* is to be fully engaged instead of trying to rush or to prolong the state of uncertainty—or, on the other hand, of procrastinating. Here is a story about how my friend Brigitta dealt with a dating *bardo*. As with so many times of uncertainty, the more we try to control a situation rather than simply be authentic, the less likely is it that things will work out. Sometimes when you stop looking and keep a "don't know" mind, the sought-after seems to find you more easily.

Brigitta went through a painful divorce when she was thirty-two. A year later, she met a man named Robert. They had some wonderful times together, and she felt intuitively that there was a deep connection. Yet the weeks went by and the relationship didn't seem to be moving forward. The uncertainty and longing caused her many sleepless nights. Then she got a job offer in another town about an hour away. She was torn: Should she stay in her old, boring job and try harder to win Robert over? Maybe her job would not be boring if she had a better relationship. Or should she move to a place where she could possibly grow in other ways and perhaps meet someone else?

Brigitta opted for the move but stayed in touch with Robert. She decided to simply allow herself to love and admire him unconditionally rather than try to control her destiny by building her life around hopes of their winding up together. A year after she let go and simply loved, he asked her to marry him, and she accepted.

Brigitta gave herself space to continue on her own path, work things through, take a breather, and settle into her own life. Despite her fears that she would spend the rest of her life alone, she used the openness of the *bardo* that her new job gave her to enrich her own life and reflect upon her wishes, needs, and priorities. She accepted the possibility that a relationship with Robert might not happen, and yet, rather than feeling negative or frustrated, she decided to objectively appreciate what a fine person he was. This is a good example of the Middle Way in what so often can be a painful and difficult experience combining longing, uncertainty, and frustrated hopes.

The secret is that we are complete and whole at every moment, even in the *bardo* state. Until we recognize and internalize this truth, life will continue to surprise and shock us. Taoist sages, Zen masters, and many ordinary people appear untouched by suffering. But in most cases, this comes only after living through a dark night of the soul and coming to terms with life's fleeting beauty, unbearable pain, and impermanence. True realized masters are not beyond suffering and dissatisfaction but are one with it.

Emergency Times

In the spring of 2009, central Italy suffered a devastating earthquake. For days, we heard the list of casualties grow as we saw on television the devastation of the beautiful, ancient towns and witnessed the desperate attempts to locate survivors. One could only imagine the horror of being trapped under the rubble. Then, when all searching was about to be suspended, ninety-eight-year-old Maria D'Antuono was discovered half buried beneath the ruins of her home, a few miles from the epicenter of the quake. She had been there for more than thirty hours. What had she been doing all that time? Her favorite pastime: crocheting.

How did she maintain her sanity without knowing whether she would ever be rescued? Crocheting was her version of meditation. It kept her aware and equanimous in any situation, in touch with what she *could* do, not wasting energy worrying about things that were out of her control.

For most of us, the horror of being imprisoned after an earthquake might seem a cruel twist of fate: "Why me?! What's going to happen to me?" Few of us might be able instead to accept the Buddhist doctrine that this is the right place, the right time, the right teaching for us, and an opportunity to surrender, releasing into whatever is to come.

Our lives are full of little *bardos* inside of bigger ones. Boredom is a *bardo*. Dating is a *bardo*. Waiting for a bus is a *bardo*. Menopause and andropause (yes, men have their own version) are *bardos*. Life itself is a *bardo*, the transitional passage between birth and death. The cluster of universes within multiverses that cosmologists and string theorists are speculating about are *bardos*. Any gap experience is a *bardo* and an opportunity for us to stay awake and aware instead of coasting. Listen to the silence between the notes. Extraordinary richness resounds therein.

MINDFUL MOMENTS

A Breathing *Bardo*

There is a momentary *bardo* between every in-breath and out-breath. See if you can experience it:

- Slowly take a breath all the way in, fill your lungs, and then hold it.
- Be aware of the fullness of the moment when your whole body is on pause; feel it in your Navel chakra, your belly, your *Hara* (below the navel): energizing, intensifying, harmonizing.

- Now, slowly and gently release your breath all the way out, and then hold it out for a few moments, having totally emptied yourself, and fully feel and experience the emptiness.
- Now, breathe in again, fully, all the way in, filling yourself up completely.
- Hold momentarily, then finally release with a great big *whoosh* or a simple *ahhh. . . .*
- Let your breathing rhythm settle, and rest lightly in the lucid present.

What did you observe? Did you stay focused throughout the whole exercise?

Pay attention to your breathing in this intentional, hyperconscious way for a few cycles. Each time, notice that tiny space between—at the turning of out-breath and before the next inhalation. Notice how it almost feels as though time stops and the space begins to feel vital, potent, and expectant.

There is a *bardo* between one thought and another, too. Can you settle into that space, letting your awareness expand and the spaciousness unfold? Are you able to feel how momentous that space is and can be? In advanced meditations, such as the Tibetan practice of *Mahamudra* or the Great Perspective, the student seeks to enter that gap between thoughts, to experience that pregnant stillness called *sunyata*. Buddhism calls this gap the "radiant womb of emptiness," a vital space in which dwell an infinite number of choices and possibilities, the alpha and omega of all experience and being.

Dreams can also unveil bardo-like glimpses of our own ever-changing, ever-emerging way of seeing and being. They point out the very transparency of what we often take to be solid and real, allowing us practice in sustaining awareness, discovering and seeing ourselves in a different light in the darkness of sleep. Dreams help us not get lost in the past, the present, or the future. Moment to moment, day to day, dreams point the way toward seeing and being in the flow of the Eternal Now. They can help us to lighten up about who we think we are, or what we think we are doing, at the moment we are dreaming. To live in the dream, appreciating the fullness, movement, and fluidity of our being, is to experience the groundless ground and be comfortable amidst uncertainty.

Movie Time as *Bardo*

Watching movies is one of my favorite *bardos*. Film, so often compared to dreaming, is like a halfway house between reality and fantasy, exemplifying the deepest perennial wisdom about our need to understand life's drama, fleeting joys, and beauty while haunted by the ever-present specter of death and change and enriched by the creative dreams of imagination, story and myth, literature, archetype, and unimaginable mystery. I savor that moment when the clear light projects onto the screen and yields a vividly magical, interwoven tale of will, wit, and woe. I love the diaphanous nature and flickering phantasmagoria of the silver screen, so akin to consciousness itself and its workings. The big screen itself is emblematic of open possibility—that is, the very emptiness or void, known to Buddhists as *sunyata,* that is the salient feature of reality, the ultimate cinema verité.

Film directors weave their magic to slow down, speed up, flash back, fast-forward, and otherwise carve up and reintegrate time into a kaleidoscopic ribbon of images, sounds, and silences. At twenty-four frames per second, the typical two-hour celluloid movie projects 172,800 separate images on the inner screens of our awareness. Yet we perceive the experience (like our selves and the years and days of our lives) as a seamless whole. Relax, sit back, and enjoy the show.

Director Alfred Hitchcock, the acknowledged master of suspense, consciously manipulated time in his films, even using timepieces as symbols (much like surrealist artist Salvador Dalí in his famous painting of a melting pocket watch). For example, in *Rope,* a dramatic film about the sensational Leopold and Loeb murder case in Chicago, actor Jimmy Stewart holds a ticking metronome in the face of the murderer, and Hitchcock's cameo in *Rear Window* is as a man winding a clock.

The movies are like a hologram or fractal of time winding and unwinding. They hold a mirror up to our own temporal and spatial elasticity. The best films, like all great art, enable us to see things in new, transcendent ways and transform our lives. What I call Film Meditation, or cinema samadhi, is a nondualistic state of consciousness in which we become one with the object we are perceiving. It can help us remain aware that it's just make-believe while we're being moved to tears or peals of joyous laughter within that cinematic minidream. This is a lesson in what Tibetan Buddhism calls Magical Body or Dream Yoga practice, which easily carries over after we exit the theater and helps us see through the illusions of everyday life.

Years ago, in one of the rare occasions when Buddhist actor Richard Gere actually spoke with his spiritual master the Dalai Lama about his career, the Dalai Lama asked him if he really felt sad or happy when he was acting and was called upon to emote in those ways. Gere said yes, adding that he had to put himself into those roles as if he were really experiencing them, and the Dalai Lama just laughed and laughed. Then he asked Gere: "How is that different than when you are not playing a special role onstage and are just playing your ordinary role in life?"

Gere said he has been reflecting on that conundrum about reality and the nature of personal identity and internal experience for the last twenty-five years!

Keep a "Don't Know" Mind

Imagine you're in an especially challenging in-between time. Now what? You can use its potential to help you choose what's next and navigate successfully through many sticky situations in life. The core of Zen Buddhist teaching is about "not knowing," or not being limited to and controlled by our personal, subjective, conceptual thoughts and egocentric feelings. Keeping a "beginner's," "original," or innocent "don't know" mind means cutting off wasteful thinking and simply centering in what is happening in the now, the only occurrence that has any truth or reality, without adding conceptual scaffolding.

The way to move forward through any *bardo*, big or small, is to set your sights on a dream or goal while maintaining that "don't know" mind. This will help keep your life in motion and help you put down roots when you are floundering. Even "not doing" is a form of doing and has its own ineluctable results. So you can set a life goal and begin to move toward it but still remain open to the possibility that something entirely different may unfold. In this way you will discover that universal consciousness beyond time and space in which all minds, hearts, and spirits are unified as one.

The secret of letting go is to let things come *and* go, and let them be. Not suppressing them or being carried away by them, but doing the best you can and then letting go. Whatever happens, according to the Five Perfections, is the right outcome for you. Or, as is stated so beautifully in Ecclesiastes: "To everything there is a season, and a time to every purpose under heaven."

Can we tolerate not knowing, and being unable to control things? Or do we mistakenly think we're in charge? Who can live on the cusp of unknowing and wonderment while in the ongoing process of simply finding out? My Zen master in Korea, KuSan Sunnim (Nine Mountains), used to ask us to contemplate this koan, or Zen riddle: *What is this? And what is this? And this?* All too often our minds become fixated, and we forget that life is fluid, in the constant process of cocreation.

Time and Time Again

I recently accompanied His Holiness the Twelfth Gyalwang Drukpa Rinpoche to New York City, where he received a prestigious United Nations Millennium Development Goal (MDG) Award for his Live to Love Foundation's ongoing humanitarian efforts in the poorest areas of the Himalayan region. The Drukpa (Dragon) Lama rarely sleeps and almost never mentions his own spiritual accomplishments (not to mention the prodigious psychic powers for which he's renowned). But one evening while we were catching up on lama gossip well into the night, he happened to mention that he'd recently discovered and ceremonially enthroned a young Tibetan boy in Boston as a *tulku* (recognized reincarnation) of Gyalwa Lorepa. This marvelously enlightened yogi master and saint of his own Drukpa Kagyu lineage had not been reborn in the last 760 years.

When I asked Rinpoche how he discovered the boy—whether from omens, dreams, Tibetan astrology, or possibly divination with dice or rosaries, as some lamas do—he told me, simply, "Meditation."

"Any special kind of meditation?" I asked, considering the many profound and esoteric skillful means such lamas are well known for.

"Luminous clarity," was all he said.

"Did you go anywhere special for that purpose?" I asked, thinking about places in Tibet, for example—perhaps a holy place, pilgrimage site, sacred cave, lake, or mountaintop where high lamas and oracles are known to have gone seeking visions about where to locate the Dalai Lama's rebirth and other grand *tulkus* of the Tibetan Buddhist hierarchy.

He just laughed, and finally said, "Not really."

"Where was that master Lorepa for the last six or seven centuries, since he passed away seven centuries ago in Tibet?" I continued, unfazed.

"Out there somewhere doing his Dharma work, no doubt," Rinpoche enigmatically replied.

I took that as a sign to press no further into these arcane spiritual mysteries of time, space, and Buddha Mind/enlightened awareness. But later I found out that the eleven-year-old Boston schoolboy was received to wide acclaim in Bhutan, after the Gyalwang Drukpa had personally recognized him and brought him back to the Indian subcontinent to continue his studies and spiritual practice. He has traded his American life for a monastery in Darjeeling to fulfill his destiny as a spiritual leader, worshipped as one of the Buddhist faith's holiest figures.

His parents say that at first they dismissed his talking about a "past life" as fantasy, but then took it seriously when he went into a trance in which he recounted the story of his former life as Gyalwa Lorepa, who died in Tibet in 1250 and was the founder of one of the main schools of Tibetan Buddhism. In the trance he also accurately described a Buddhist monastery with a thirty-five-foot dragon on its roof—a place he had never visited.

When asked if he would like to go back to Boston, the boy said that he wants to stay and fulfill his responsibilities. "I will miss my school days, but I am happy in my new role. I like it here," he said.

In Buddhism, reincarnation is the eternal process of coming into being and evolving (though occasionally backsliding) while trying over and over to complete our lessons here, in the classroom of our lives. Each lifetime is an opportunity to "clean house," as it were, and to make better choices, thus enhancing and maturing our spiritual consciousness. Buddha himself said, regarding rebirth and karmic unfolding: "If you wish to know what your past lives were like, look at how you are now. If you want to know about your future lives, look at what you're doing and being right now."

From a Buddhist perspective, reincarnation is the cycle of growth and learning across many lifetimes. Whether or not we believe in reincarnation, the concept offers tremendous opportunities for reflection and self-development. The endless flow of time is a powerful lens through which to examine the patterns of our life and discover that we, our choices included, are not fixed. Our stories—our lives—evolve. We make mistakes but don't have to be defined by those mistakes. Our lives don't suddenly stop when we achieve a major life goal, nor should they. Life flows on, in a myriad of forms and ways. Here are some ways we can delve more deeply into an understanding of the fluidity and movement that surround our moments and days.

- We can examine our past to reframe our history, discover what is true, free ourselves from unhelpful stories and scripts, and create a positive lineage of strength, caring, and wisdom for those who come after us.

- We can recognize that we are the result of our past, both individually and collectively.

- We can see that our present actions reach forward and have implications for the future, in this life and in subsequent ones.

- We can understand that our actions affect not only ourselves, but also others around us and their futures as well; our actions also affect the entire environment, of which we are each a significant part.

- We can therefore gain a new respect for the import of each thought, intention, word, deed, and relationship, in each moment, because these are the fertile seeds of the future. An action when repeated can become a pattern, then an ingrained habit, and defines character, karma, and destiny.

As Buddhism and other great faiths teach, at the deepest level the personal and the planetary are indivisible. Understanding larger cycles and rhythms of time will help us lead more balanced, fulfilling lives as our own days and years unfold. As we all intuitively know, time is speeding up. On one level, we all experience this in our own lives. Summer vacation seems to last forever when we are young, for example, but when we are middle-aged it whizzes by in the blink of an eye. As you've no doubt noticed, our notion and perception of time changes as we get older. This could be because a day or a year is a much smaller percentage of our life as we grow older, and so feels shorter. Similarly, on a larger scale, with an overview of world history it has been posited that time itself is literally accelerating.

In *One Peaceful World: Creating a Healthy and Harmonious Mind, Home, and World Community,* educator Michio Kushi envisions history as a giant spiral or chambered nautilus. The hours unwind like a clock. The twelve segments (see diagram) are not equal but, because the spiral is logarithmic, grow increasingly smaller in size and shorter in duration. The first sections span over a thousand years, whereas the last section extends less than fifty years.

Because of the spiraling nature of historical development, history actually does repeat itself to a degree. For instance, the time of intense war activity marked by the Crusades and the Mongol invasions a millennia ago occurs at the same point in its era as do World Wars I and II in ours. In the same way, the age of discovery that saw contact established between East and West and between the Old World and the New World falls in the same section of its era as does the modern space age, which saw the launching of the first earth satellites and the landing on the moon.

Each orbit of the spiral is approximately one-third as long as the previous one. In other words, each period changes at three times the speed of the previous age. Historically, the change of society as well as the development of technology and consciousness have accelerated exponentially. For example, within historical times the use of fire has increased at a geometrical ratio as

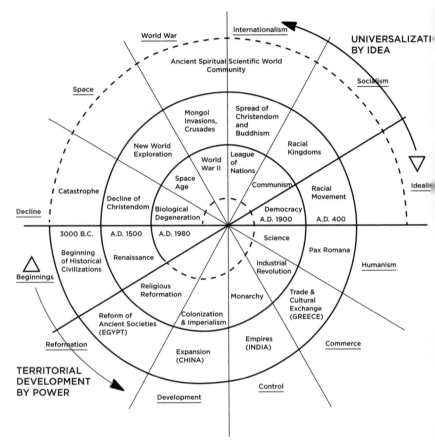

THE GREAT WHEEL OF TIME

the source of cooking fuel, home heating fuel, metallurgical energy, and other technological energy changed from wood to charcoal (about three thousand years), from charcoal to coal (about one thousand years), from coal to petroleum (about three hundred years), from petroleum to electricity (about a hundred years), and from electricity to nuclear power (about thirty years).

The next twenty-five or thirty years—shown in the center of the drawing by the short semicircular dotted line at the top—will be the time of greatest contraction, as we pass through the center of the historical spiral going back thousands of years. High pressure governs our current era, the latest orbit of which began in approximately 1980. High pressure is manifested as follows:

1. High speed (rapid advances in transportation, communications, and sequencing DNA)

2. High production (increased mechanization and consumption)

3. High efficiency (the introduction of computers, robotics, and cell phones)

4. High metabolism and increased nutrient intake (the global spread of high-calorie, high-protein, high-fat, high-sugar diets)

5. Rapid movement (fast circulation of people, money, and information)

Under this accelerating pressure, many things are exceeding their levels of tolerance and are beginning to disintegrate: the climate and environment, the financial system and other institutions of society, the family structure, the mental and psychological stability of people, and the cellular stability of organs, tissues, and cells.

In the period ahead, all aspects of human affairs—religious and scientific, political and economic, social and cultural, national and international, individual and universal, material and spiritual, climatic and environmental—will converge as the spiral of history accelerates. This age will be the most confused, complicated, competitive, and condensed period that humanity has ever experienced. It is governed largely by artificialization at all levels: food, energy, medicine, art, technology, and ideologies.

However, as the present centripetal spiral ends, a new centrifugal spiral has already started to form within the old. A new era is now dawning, its seeds quickening for thousands of years in the teachings of Moses, Buddha, Lao-tzu, Confucius, Jesus, Muhammad, Hildegard of Bingen, Rumi, Susan B. Anthony, Gandhi, Martin Luther King, the Dalai Lama, Nelson Mandela,

Thich Nhat Hanh, Desmond Tutu, and other prophets of humanity. This countertendency is also gaining momentum and can be described as natural, organic, sustainable, holistic, cooperative, and spiritual. There is the potential for the beginning of a new cycle of peace and harmony that could lead to our cocreation of an enlightened planet and endure for thousands of years.

The possibility of contributing to this awakening is inherent in every moment.

A Planetary Tune-up

The more aware we become of energy, our own and others', the more we also tune in to the energy of the earth. Tying together the upper and lower, sacred and profane, cosmic and quotidian, male and female—in brief, harmonizing all the polarities in life—is the essence of realizing our full potential as human beings. And by balancing or healing ourselves, we can help heal the world.

Recent research suggests that the earth's main frequency is changing. Scientists report that the Schumann resonances—electromagnetic waves that have been identified as the earth's natural frequencies—are now rising in frequency, potentially endangering the entire biosphere. Like global warming, the primary cause of this elevation appears to be human activity. Specifically, the tremendous increase in artificial electromagnetic radiation from satellites, cell phones, computers, televisions, and other military and civilian electronic devices and communications networks is overshadowing the earth's steady pulse of 7.83 hertz. Electropollution depresses the immune function, increases stress and fatigue, and contributes to further physical, emotional, and mental imbalance. We are growing more and more out of tune with nature and the cosmos.

To help restore equilibrium, it is important to avoid or minimize the use of artificial electromagnetic radiation. There are a variety of small portable resonators that simulate the Schumann resonances that can be used in the home or office. But the best way to restore harmony with the planet and to normalize your own personal circadian rhythms is to meditate regularly. As research shows, meditation generates a cascade of alpha, theta, and gamma rhythms through the brain and central nervous system, flooding all the chakras, meridians, organs, tissues, and cells with a healthful, vital energy. Just several minutes of contemplation a day—beginning with the basic "Breathe, Smile, Relax" exercise followed by a short mindfulness or presencing meditation—will plug you into the earth's natural frequency, reset your inner clock, and renew and refresh you for the entire day. And just as the planet's rhythmic pulse will help unify your body, mind, and spirit, the vibration you create will help sustain the earth and its extraordinary biodiversity. Modern science has now shown empirically what ancient Buddhist wisdom long ago proclaimed: all sentient beings are attuned to the same frequency.

Imagine, if you will, what it might be like to leave the confusion and stress of daily life one day, walk out your door, and have an epiphany—a glorious vision of time like a shining wheel before you. Imagine yourself experiencing a revelation not only about the spiral of history but also about the origin of the cosmos, the creation of our planet, and the workings of our solar system, galaxy, and universe, suddenly radiant and clear in your mind.

Not like a science program on high-definition TV, a 3-D Hollywood movie, or a virtual-reality experience. Instead, a blinding realization about how everything fits together—and, significantly, your destined, meaningful part in all of it. Imagine yourself suddenly understanding how the energy of the human body flows, with all of its functions and processes, including gestation and birth and the different levels of consciousness. Imagine yourself suddenly understanding how your spiritual mind works and is a part of, and inseparable from, the universal consciousness of Buddha

Mind. Imagine yourself getting a brief glimpse of that finely calibrated and jewel-like cosmic clockwork here in earthly time and space.

And then imagine being transformed as you finally understand how everything fits together. How just being here makes perfect, divine sense. This vision is one of the most highly guarded esoteric teachings of Tibetan Buddhism. It is an image of the *Kalachakra*, the Great Wheel of Time that spirals out from the deepest recesses of our spiritual mind and enfolds and activates us and underlies all our experiences. In fact, the experience I describe has been reenacted in an esoteric Tantric initiation ceremony for thousands of years. One of the greatest gifts of the Dalai Lama has been to share the power of the *Kalachakra* with the world, a mission to bring us back into balance and help foster world peace.

To prepare for the initiation ceremony of the *Kalachakra*, a select group of highly trained monks spends a period of about three weeks painstakingly creating on a horizontal surface—symbolic of the boundless expanse of time and space—a mandala wheel nearly seven feet in diameter out of finely ground stone that is richly colored with pigments. As the monks work, their prayers, that living energy of attention, go grain by grain into the extremely intricate and vivid powder design of 722 deities—which are different manifestations of the supreme meditational deity Kalachakra—along with Sanskrit symbols; sacred implements; human, animal, and plant figures; and other mystical elements.

When the mandala is finished, it serves as a highly charged vortex of living energy manifested through the devoted prayers, chants, visualizations, and concentrated meditations of the monks. It is a microcosmic representation of sacred time and sacred space. To take part in the creation of the *Kalachakra*, through all of those minutes, hours, days, and weeks, is to become the marvelous Wheel itself.

What more powerful cosmic tune-up could there be? Not only for the monks. Not only for those students for whom viewing the mandala is the culmination of a twelve-day preparation to receive the teaching and contemplative experience of the initiation ceremony that follows, but for everyone who is touched consciously or unconsciously by its vibrations.

The Dalai Lama explains: "It is a way of planting a seed, and the seed will have karmic effect. One doesn't need to be present at the *Kalachakra* ceremony in order to receive its benefits." The ceremony, with all of its accumulated energy, is a gift to the whole world. His Holiness has performed this ceremony as a blessing and peace offering on dozens of occasions during his life, at crucial times and places in the world, chosen according to Tibetan Buddhist astrology and divination.

The *Kalachakra* mandala has been created in places as diverse as Madison Square Garden in New York City; Barcelona; Toronto; Sydney, Australia; Bloomington, Indiana; and Madison, Wisconsin; as well as in numerous locations in India and Nepal. I myself experienced this cosmic empowerment from the Dalai Lama in Bodh Gaya near the Bodhi Tree, along with a throng of native people, in 1974. At the end of the viewing time, which can last for several weeks, there is a deconsecration ceremony. The entire sacred artwork is destroyed—another lesson in impermanence and nonattachment. The sand is swept up, put in a jar, and then poured into a local body of water to disperse and spread blessings throughout the universe.

Thus in each creation of this deep mystery, the Great Wheel of Time floods the world with a powerful transmission of prayerful energy. Let us find peace and make peace, *become* peace—for the benefit of one and all.

To some, the *Kalachakra* might seem like an interesting cultural artifact. But it can remind us to sweep up the best grains of our lives, marshal our best intentions, and, through the supreme power of enlightened mind, send them as seeds of healing energy out into the world and the future.

Breathing In the Future, Breathing Out the Past

Raise your arms,

now lower them.

Breathe in while raising arms,

breathe out while lowering. Again,

breathing in while raising,

breathing out while lowering.

Breathe in and raise your arms, filling up

and stimulating, energizing, filling, expanding;

breathing out and lowering, emptying out, decreasing, dissolving.

Breathing in and filling, raising,

breathing in the future and hope;

breathing out and lowering, letting go of the past,

dissolving and disappearing,

grounding yourself in the present.

Breathing in and filling the whole universe,

one great sphere of totality, and breathing out while lowering and

dissolving.

Breathe in and raise your arms, filling up

and stimulating, energizing, filling, expanding;

breathing out and lowering, emptying out, decreasing, dissolving.

Breathing in and filling, raising,

breathing in future lives and hope;

breathing out past lives and letting go of all past disappointments,

regrets, and concerns, all dissolving and disappearing.

Breathing in and raising up, filling up the whole universe,

and breathing out while lowering the arms,

relaxing, dissolving, letting go, and letting be.

Losing yourself,

finding your true Self,
rest in luminous, centerless openness as your breath
gently returns to normal
and you savor the incandescent moment
of nowness-awareness,
at home with yourself,
nakedly being, just being
free and complete.

The age we live in is itself a *bardo*—a time of great uncertainty between thousands of generations of relative sustainability and the future of Homo sapiens on this planet. Will we survive? It is by no means certain. In this time of shocking, constant, and unpredictable change, we are faced with the possibility that human life on earth may not be tenable a century or less from now. We can go our separate, individual ways and live for our own personal enjoyment. Or we can combine our collective energies and cocreate a "Global Time Zone." Instead of racing one another down a track to temporary riches and the illusions of security, we can share in the knowledge that, in the fullness of time, with our wonderful modern technology, communication, transportation, and other products of our ingenuity, there is more than enough for all. We can choose to become the mindful planetary stewards and wise children and sage elders we wish to see in this world, for the benefit of present and future generations.

The truth is that this is the world we are promised, this is the promised land—when we are genuinely awake to it. This earth is like an altar, and we are the gods and goddesses upon it. I firmly believe that it is incumbent upon to us to live and act accordingly, for the benefit of ourselves and the generations to come. Do we really have another viable choice?

When asked by a visiting student to describe Buddhism in two words, Suzuki Roshi famously said, "Everything changes." Today time and change are both accelerating, and we are at a crossroads in human development. For a more peaceful, harmonious, and joyful collective existence to flourish, Buddhist wisdom reminds us that compassion must be expressed as loving-kindness in action. For our global environment and society, we promote an altruistic, reciprocal, and interconnected attitude of heart. As the Dalai Lama recently said, "Help develop world peace through cultivating inner peace along with altruistic social engagement and compassionate action. Take responsibility now for a better and safer world."

The time is right for positive, intentional change, and every moment presents a point of choice. If not you, who? And if not now, when?

CONCLUSION:
THE INFINITE POSSIBILITIES OF NOW

YOU MAY HAVE PICKED up this book while you were not having a good relationship with time, while you were feeling overwhelmed and rushed and finding it impossible to get everything done that you needed to each day. I hope and trust that you now have a fuller understanding of time itself and of how you can have a gentler, more harmonious and optimistic alliance with it. Mick Jagger was right: time *is* on your side. As you incorporate compassionate mindfulness and meditation techniques into your life and live according to the Buddhist principles of nowness-awareness, balance, and loving-kindness, you'll find yourself able to make the most of every moment—no longer time's victim, but its friendly partner and cocreator. You can experience for yourself the joys of life in Buddha Standard Time.

I compare living in Buddha Standard Time to riding a bicycle; it may be difficult at first, but eventually you do it instinctively, making constant, almost imperceptible shifts and adjustments in balance, rather than maintaining rigidity, as you maneuver along the ever-changing terrain. In addition to being aware of energy and polarities, this involves being ever mindful of thought, intention, word, and deed, and their karmic resonances. The more mindful you become, the better you will be able to cycle with intention, purpose, and clarity. Deepening and refining your awareness so that you can live completely in Buddha Standard Time is something to experiment with and play with your entire life (or lives). You will be gratified by all the benefits you reap. Think of Dorothy in the movie version of *The Wizard of Oz* and how when she landed in Oz, everything bloomed in vivid color. In training your mind, your perception of life becomes incredibly rich and vibrant. You come out of the flatlands into multidimensional worlds of genuine relationship, sense, and spirit.

Another term for living fully and completely in Buddha Standard Time—using mindfulness, meditation, nowness-awareness, and compassion—is *enlightenment*. It is a tall spiritual order, but it is within your grasp. And from the personal to the planetary, it raises our happiness quotient and collective well-being.

Some people feel that you need to strive for enlightenment, and not just now, but even for many lifetimes. Others say that working to achieve it runs counter to actually obtaining it, for too much emphasis on a goal obscures the reality right here and now. Although these are just conceptual ways of thinking, I myself tend to favor the more nondualistic approach of the Middle Way. It balances contentment where you are with Right Effort, and radical acceptance with a compassionate commitment to spiritual transformation on both the individual and the collective level. I call this "being there while getting there, every single step of the way."

Enlightened living is not an either-or proposition in which you are either enlightened or you are not. Traditionally, it's taught that there are levels of enlightenment and awareness, and that we touch into them at different points along the way until our cosmic awareness is totally realized and stabilized; at that point there is no backsliding. This is known as unexcelled perfect and total enlightenment. Yet even one moment of true awareness and transparency is a moment of complete freedom and enlightenment, as I myself can attest, as the scriptures corroborate, and as I hope you yourself understand after reading this book. We can enter Buddha Standard Time at any moment. We do not have to wait for some messiahlike enlightenment experience but can usher in the heavenly realm of nirvana right here and now, through awakened awareness; this is our birthright and also our legacy to future generations, to the extent that we can uphold and stand up for it.

When you make peace with time, and are not hurried and harried, you will find that room mysteriously opens up for new possibilities. Each moment is a doorway to the divine state of grace. Patience is a facet of the jewel of love, allowing enough time to create intimacy in relationships rather than experience them as ships passing in the night, which rushing through life is likely to give you instead. Mental calm, centeredness, and clarity provide a healing, nourishing pause in the frantic activity of our lives. Meher Baba, a renowned South Indian saint of the last century, often used to say (on a chalkboard, since he kept silent for decades), "A mind that is too fast and jumpy is sick. A slow and steady and stable mind is sound. A mind that is still is divine."

Some people believe in an afterlife full of angels and loving spirits. But there are angels/bodhisattvas here right now, among us and even within us. And you can learn to experience the timeless in every instant—heaven on earth. You can give your blessings and benedictions to all those you meet. You can greet the golden sun in the early morning, water the plants, put out nuts and seeds for the squirrels and birds, feel compassion for friends and strangers, forgive those who have wronged you, give alms to beggars and smiles to whomever you happen to encounter, contribute time and money to worthy causes, nurture your local community and protect the environment, and send peaceful thoughts to global trouble spots. You will be calming yourself as well as sending out waves of loving-kindness and good wishes. This royal generosity is extraordinarily rewarding. What greater gift can you give yourself and the world?

This moment, right now, is perfect, the golden eternity. It's up to you to claim it and make yourself at home in it, using it wisely. Luxuriate in the space between thoughts, in the transitions between activities, creating little oases of peace wherever you may be, regardless of your outer circumstances. This is spiritual freedom and autonomy—what the medieval mystics called "honorable rest." You deserve it.

I would like to leave you with ten thoughts to help you live in Buddha Standard Time for all the moments, days, and years of your life.

Ten Tips and Pointers for Befriending Time

1. Rest in the breath while letting go of all thoughts, concerns, plans, worries, and preoccupations.

2. Be mindful of the physical sensations you feel right now.

3. Feel the good earth beneath your feet or the seat that cradles you.

4. Chant a mantra or sacred phrase again and again, with pure, undivided concentration and focus.

5. Make eye contact with another being, and feel compassion and lovingkindness for whomever you are with.

6. Smile at someone, hug someone, or help someone.

7. Go outside and make contact with nature through the sky, clouds, trees, a flower, a body of water, the earth between your fingers, or any other manifestation of the magnificent natural world.

8. Read sacred words from the world's wisdom traditions and scriptures

9. Take a break, a sacred pause, an "honorable rest"—whether for Sabbath or just for an hour or two—at least once a week, if not every day.

10. Listen to music, sing, dance, create, pray, and play.

Now breathe, smile, and relax . . . You have time.

ACKNOWLEDGMENTS

HERE IS THE PERFECT time and place to thank the right people for their excellent and generous hands in helping with this book project. First, I want to thank an extraordinary team—my editor, Gideon Weil, and my literary agent, Susan Lee Cohen—without whom this book would not have come into being. Also Alex Jack, Rondi Lightmark, Linda Carbone, and Alice Peck for their patient helping hands. Plus Maria Schulman, Carl Walesa, Carolyn Holland, Professor Leslie McLain, Christopher and Daniela Coriat, and Roz and Dan Stark for assisting in this process; and my wonderful assistant Kathleen Albanese.

May all goodness and joy be theirs as they enjoy all the time in the world.

ABOUT DZOGCHEN CENTER

Lama Surya Das founded Dzogchen Center with Nyoshul Khenpo Rinpoche in 1991 to further the transmission of Buddhist contemplative practices and mindful living to Western audiences along with the transformation of these teachings into effective forms that help to alleviate suffering and further a civilization based on wisdom and compassion.

The Dzogchen Center website, www.dzogchen.org, is a regularly updated resource for Dzogchen Center information, teaching and retreat schedules, local meditation groups, podcasts, and online registration Information can also be found at www.surya.org.

 DZOGCHEN CENTER

P.O. Box 340459

Austin, TX 78734

Phone: (617) 628-1702

E-mail: info@dzogchen.org